6·19

a beautiful
journey

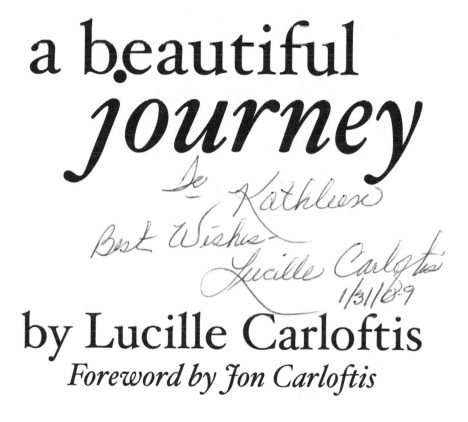

To Kathleen
Best Wishes
Lucille Carloftis
1/31/8-9

by Lucille Carloftis
Foreword by Jon Carloftis

Acclaim Press
Your Next Great Book

MORLEY, MISSOURI

Acclaim Press
Your Next Great Book

P.O. Box 238
Morley, Missouri 63767
(573) 472-9800
www.acclaimpress.com

Additional copies may be purchased directly from
Acclaim Press, Inc.

Library of Congress Control Number: 2007937081

ISBN-10: 0-9798802-4-6
ISBN-13: 978-0-9798802-4-7

0 9 8 7 6 5 4 3 2 1

Contents

Dedication

Carlo and Lucille Carloftis

Dedicated to
Carlo and our children.

Foreword

Jon Carloftis

Surely, when my parents left a beautiful home to begin a new life on the banks of the Rockcastle River without electricity, water, TV, or many other "necessities", people thought they were crazy. But they had a dream: to live a life, with their children and each other, surrounded by nature.

There were times growing up when I thought we were missing out on some of the "normal" activities that most people lived through like their Dads golfing, their Mothers playing bridge, television...but even then, we knew that we were living a very special life.

Our childhood consisted of meeting new people everyday, playing on the river with swinging grapevines, fishing, canoeing, hiking, playing with the Cherokee children that lived on the property during the summer, playing cowboys and Indians in our own little replica of a pioneer town complete with a paddle-wheel boat, a horse-drawn surrey, and all the animals that were dropped off at our place because people knew we would find a home for them...we didn't know it, but our life was so rich! Thank goodness our parents provided this amazing childhood for us. It has certainly made me feel that anything on Earth is possible with noble intentions and hard work.

I am speaking for my brothers and sisters when I say that no other possible childhood could have been more exciting (except maybe, Indiana Jones) than ours on the Rockcastle River. Momma and Daddy...thank you, thank you, thank you.

Jon Carloftis
Author of *First a Garden* and *Beyond the Window Sill*

Introduction

Lucille Bowling Carloftis, is without doubt, a wonderful storyteller who has the ability to turn the mundane into the extraordinary. Her choice of descriptors for her characters afford them human, unforgettable personal qualities. These characters could be met on the streets of a city or on country roads. The settings are absolutely poetry in prose. She is able to transport the reader from the cobblestone streets of St. Augustine, Florida, to the banks of the Rockcastle River in rural Kentucky in the flash of an eye and never "skip a beat." This book reveals the most meaningful experiences of her life, and the richness she has derived from them by being a fellow traveler. Lucille and *A Beautiful Journey* are inexorably bound together.

Lucille "waltzed" into my life more than six decades ago, and little did 1 know then that she would become my life-long friend. She was the new girl in Manchester Elementary School, and everyone noticed her as she quickly joined them jumping the rope at recess. She was wearing a striking coral and white playsuit, designed and made by her mother and grandmother who were truly artists in their own professions. Her bouncing black curls and hazel eyes were strikingly beautiful, but those eyes could not disguise the slight mischief shown in her every movement. Her whole demeanor seemed to say, "1 know things. Come with me, and 1 will share them with you." Strangely enough, she was immediately accepted by everyone, and never regarded with the suspicions that often accompany the unfamiliar newcomer to the mountains of southeastern Kentucky. We simply wanted to know her better.

Many years have passed since Lucille's first day of school in Manchester Elementary, and she has experienced her fair share of joys and sorrows. Whether ecstatic with happiness or devastated with sorrow, she has quickly rebounded with her never-failing tranquility because she is a survivor. As the visitor enters her shop, or her home, he or she is greeted with the warmest of smiles and given the feeling of being special. These visitors return again and again, year after year.

The reader of *A Beautiful Journey* will become the visitors due to memorable characters, and scenes depicted on every page. As an old admirer of hers once remarked, "You, sir, are in the presence of a lady-a very gracious lady." You, the reader, will certainly know this.

Jean Baker Cobb

a beautiful *journey*

The Dream Began

*O*utside my bedroom window I have a marvelous view. On clear evenings I turn out the lights and then watch the huge mother-of-pearl moon rise far above the hills and beyond. There's a brief moment when the river catches its reflection and magnifies the moon's brightness. As I stand at the window and gaze at such splendor, I often feel as if this grand performance has been rolled out just for me.

Rockcastle River runs about a hundred miles through the Daniel Boone National Forest. It was discovered in 1674 by Gabriel Arthur, who was captured, then released by the Shawnee Indians. A Civil War battle was fought nearby at Camp Wildcat. The river's character changes from season to season and sometimes even from day to day—slow-moving, crystal-clear summer pools give way to angry, brown fall floods which push its waters through the trees, sometimes forty to fifty feet higher than normal. The river changes color too, from light brown to aquamarine to deep emerald.

Carlo and I built an Indian village here in 1955, right on the banks of the Rockcastle River in the foothills of Appalachia. A narrow, park-like ribbon of land stretched nearly a mile between the river and the highway. In some spots the river dropped deeper and then flooded during the early spring rains. Views were limited, just a small angular valley with foliage on both sides. Closed off from the dangers and intrusions of the outside world, it was an ideal place, we thought, to start our new business.

Carlo grew up in Pineville, a small community town on the Cumberland River in southeastern Kentucky. His mother was Appalachian, and his stepfather, George Karloftis was a colorful, flamboyant immigrant from Patrico, Greece. With Carlo and his younger brother Floyd, they moved to Pineville in 1927 and together opened the Hub Grill, a restaurant that remained a popular establishment for decades. It sat on a corner, right across from the Courthouse and was consistently successful in serving tasty food to this well-ordered town made up of several different cultural backgrounds—and to surrounding areas as well.

Like most small towns, Pineville was steeped in friendliness. It never failed to generate hospitality. On sunny afternoons in the late 1940s, four of us young mothers gathered with our babies in their buggies and strolled the wide sidewalks, visiting with neighbors who lounged on their front porches and surveyed their manicured lawns. Afterward we stopped at the Hub Grill for iced tea and Cokes. And, in season, luscious, red-ripe watermelon.

The town changed, as all towns do in time. The Continental Hotel with its railings and sweeping porches is no longer there, nor are the fancy dress shops, Mary's and Miss Mabel's. But the beautiful churches and homes are, and for the most part, inhabited by the same families that Carlo knew as a young boy in the 1920s, racing up and down the streets on his roller skates, wearing his Popeye sweater, delivering the Knoxville *News Journal* before rushing off to school. On his way he stopped at various service stations and dipped his skates into barrels of used motor oil, giving them a smoother, quicker ride. By the time he arrived at Pineville Elementary, though, classes had already started.

By high school age Carlo was thinking pretty highly of himself as a romancer—dating and dancing with all the pretty girls at Brookings, the hangout for young people. One of the local beauties, it turned out, was Marilyn Monroe's half-sister, Bernice Baker, from the Wallsend section of town.

His college career ended before the first semester even began. His family had never put a lot of emphasis on higher education. They believed that the path to success and riches lay in hard work. And for them it did. For Carlo, though, it was either work, work, work or play, play, play. Yet he often seemed to be unable to balance the two, so for several years his life was without pattern or purpose—until he began to follow his own dream.

Despite its many changes, Pineville still has an interesting distinction: There's a looming chained rock that hangs above it, and it's home not only to Kentucky's first state park, but also to the Mountain Laurel Festival, a showy event that began in the early 1930s and still attracts high school and college students from all over the state.

It's also where Carlo and I first met.

I had come from a long line of artistic people. My mother and grandmother, both excellent seamstresses, could open a box and pull out swatches of silks, linens and lace and create beautiful clothing. My grandmother also hand-loomed rugs that cascaded over the backs of chairs and down onto the wood floors. Sometimes I fell asleep to the steady hum of the sewing machine. They had it just right. They loved what they were doing, and I developed an early appreciation for their work.

When the sun shone through the windows in the early morning, a new day had begun for their creativity and reading pleasure. My blind uncle, imprisoned in a world of darkness since before age two, sat in his upstairs bedroom and entertained us with his Appalachian-style fiddle playing.

I had spent most of my young life away from Mama, a schoolteacher who had once taught her brother Chester to read Braille. She had suffered a long illness from an injury she had received from being thrown from a horse as a young girl. Unable to care for me, Daddy took me to his mother's home—and it was there that I stayed. By age twelve, though, I was eager for Mama to join us. She had never lost her courageous, soft-spoken ways, nor did she depart from her quiet reserve in telling me how to behave. While Mama was teaching me the art of being a lady, to mind my manners and hold my head up, Grandma was reading aloud some interesting tidbit she had just run across, instructing me in the value of good eating habits, and to keep my dress down.

Growing up with my grandmother in Manchester, there was something new to learn every day, although at the time I didn't realize it. There were few rules—to come to the breakfast table not completely dressed and groomed for the day would have been an unspeakable crime—but no shortage of love. There's one thing I know: I was a very lucky girl. Years later I would tell my grandmother, who was ninety at the time, that I wished she could come and help me raise my own children. She simply declared, "Grandma's too old now."

Yet, after finishing high school, I walked out of this quiet, peaceful, modest but orderly home, lit with dangling 60-watt bulbs, and got married.

Four years earlier, my grandmother and I traveled to Pineville to visit my half sister Beatrice. We walked into the Hub Grill. Carlo, standing behind the kitchen's swinging doors with Floyd, peered through the glass, spotted me, then jabbed his brother in the ribs and demanded, "Who's that?" Floyd didn't know. "On second thought," Carlo said, "she's going to be my wife someday." ("On second thought," I would learn later, was one of his favorite phrases.) "You're crazy," Floyd retorted.

So Carlo walked out and introduced himself. I thought he was as handsome as any movie star, dark and tan, with such refined, charming manners. But he was twenty-eight years old. I was only fifteen.

Back in Manchester, to my astonishment, he began showing up. He'd drop in at the drugstore where I worked the soda fountain. He'd order something small, then smile and leave. Or I'd be practicing cheers for our high school's basketball game, and I'd look up, and he'd be there. That spring, he sent me an orchid corsage for Easter. I went frolicking in a grassy meadow, looking for colored eggs, wearing it pinned to my shoulder.

After I turned nineteen, Carlo's mother, who was ill, wanted to see me. So I traveled to Pineville for a short visit. Or so I thought. Soon after my arrival, Carlo proposed. I accepted—and we were married very simply at around 5:00 p.m. in his mother's upstairs bedroom, where she lay, propped up on pillows. Our only guests were her friends, Asher and Rose Arnett and Bo and Louise Combs. Irene, his mother's grandniece, was also present.

Instead of going on a honeymoon, we set off for the main square uptown to celebrate. We swept along the sidewalks and darted in and out of cafe doors as Carlo introduced me as his new bride to everyone in sight. It was definitely high drama. We were greeted with effusive affection by his old friends, who leaned out of windows to watch as we left to go to the next place. Only later did I learn that some were already predicting that our marriage wouldn't last six weeks. They couldn't have known that we were about to embark on an exciting life filled with adventure.

When I returned to Manchester in January, 1948, as a married woman, my parents were stunned, to put it mildly. My grandmother, with characteristic bluntness, asked my new husband, "What do you want with this child?" But Carlo's mother was ecstatic. She thought I would bring out the best in him.

So my life changed. The Carloftises were businesspeople, operating what was for that time an upscale restaurant. Everything was hurry-and-go, open twenty hours, seven days a week. Mama would hardly pick up a needle on Sunday. The Hub Grill had so many quality food selections that I felt overwhelmed. Chef Steve was Greek and cooked traditional dishes, but it was Chloe "Ma" Stuart who brought real style to the kitchen. Everything about her was voluptuous, from her big, beautiful hats to her pastries and pies. She believed in using only the finest ingredients. She'd worked at Colonel Sanders Café for a while, and it was thought by some that she was instrumental in developing his secret, world-famous fried chicken recipe.

Waiters, hurried yet smiling, came out of the kitchen carrying heavy trays filled with delicious dishes to a room full of people, both locals and the courthouse crowd. In the evenings, the sophisticated and fashionably dressed sat near the big window up front. I enjoyed the bustling—and the good food. But even I had no idea until decades later of just how far the Hub's hospitality extended.

It was Memorial Day, 2005. My son Buzz and I decided that after attending church services in Livingston we would drive over to Pineville to place flowers on friends' and family members' graves. When we arrived, I noticed the black Bethel Baptist Church was still in session. Pulling into the parking lot, I asked the ladies and gentlemen standing nearby if Joyce Whitley, a former Hub Grill employee, happened to be inside. She was.

Then I spotted Kat Cloud, another former employee, moving slowly down the front steps. Also dependent on her cane, she was still a very elegant lady. She greeted us with delight and invited us to come inside. Buzz hesitated; he was dressed in shorts, sandals and a logoed t-shirt, somewhat inappropriate among such finely dressed churchgoers. But the gentlemen managed to convince him that God didn't care what he wore, so he agreed—and we enjoyed a delicious dinner, along with a sanctuary service afterward, where the congregation sang and clapped and the pastor moved rhythmically with the music up the aisle. "Well," Buzz remarked, "they certainly know how to make visitors feel warmly welcomed."

But the best surprise was still to come. Before we left, Kat told me a story: A visiting evangelist from Knoxville had revealed that as a young man in Pineville he'd been known as the town drunk. Nevertheless, each day a plate of hot food was set out for him near the Hub Grill's back door—by Kat herself. Christian charity could hardly have gone farther. I felt proud that Carlo's family business was still so fondly remembered.

Still, as a young bride in 1948, I missed our dining room back home, with its round oak table, covered with crisp white linen and set with my grandmother's blue willow china. So for her seventy-fifth birthday (she would live to be 101), I traveled back to Manchester to help celebrate. I invited "Ma" to go along. She was living at the Carloftis home, as I would later learn was customary for close friends who worked at the Hub Grill.

I walked through the house's long hall to where she was standing. A very handsome lady, I thought, who clearly knew the rules of etiquette. She wore her usual chic costume of gloves and a huge hat.

She took one look at me in my plain, simple attire and declared, "You can't go back home looking like that. Straighten up and throw back your shoulders and look like you have at least married into something." She raised her eyebrows for emphasis. No wonder her great-granddaughters would become the famous Wrigley Chewing Gum twins on TV commercials. "Ma" knew style, and I had only the basics. But a few little touches here and there would fix that.

First she fastened Carlo's mother's beautiful diamond watch bracelet around my wrist. Then she draped her mink stole across my shoulders. Before walking out of the door to get into their car, a creamy yellow Chrysler with a striking red plaid interior, the ultimate in luxury with a handsome sporty look, I could see I had captured both their attention and full approval.

A birthday cake was in the trunk, ready to go. We waved our goodbyes and headed in the direction of Manchester. I was glad to be home again with my family and to sit in the comfort and warmth of our fireplace. Pineville now seemed very far away. The party soon ended with an informal and unplanned charm. It had been fun.

But now it was late afternoon and time to leave. We drove to London, a distance of some thirty miles and decided to stop at the Krystal Kitchen for something to drink. This was long before the convenience of drive-throughs. We parked alongside the curb. We went inside, plunked down into a booth and were served refreshing soft drinks. Then I looked inside my purse to pay—but no! In my flurry of getting properly dressed, I had switched handbags. "Ma" had left her money at home too. I was mortified and wanted to crawl under the table. But then "Ma" declared, "I guess we will just have to wash the dishes." Laughing, she kept digging in her handbag, and finally found a package of three cent postage stamps. We paid the cashier in stamps and left.

I was now a wife—and eventually, a mother. Our daughter Carcille was born in 1949. She was joined in 1951 by our son Buzz, in 1953 and 1955 by daughters Koula and Betsy, and in 1960 and 1964 by sons Dusty and Jon. Carlo, it turned out, was a wonderful husband and a devoted father. When Carcille was a baby, in fact, he insisted on preparing her formula himself, and over the years, with all six children, he took far more than his share of the nighttime feedings.

Carlo understood every phase of the restaurant business, from peeling onions to cooking and serving to the most discriminating tastes. He and Floyd were expected to take over the Hub Grill someday. But my husband had an adventurous spirit, an entrepreneurial urge, a desire to explore and examine life in another locale, to move beyond what he already knew. We would talk in whispers late at night. I can still hear his mother's voice calling from her upstairs bedroom, "Carlo, quit building air castles!"

What she didn't realize was that because I loved him, I shared his passion.

Outdoor theaters were beginning to catch on across the country, and since there was only one in our area, we decided to build another. Well, easier said than done. First we needed a building permit—so we joined a parade of others who were also waiting in line. Finally, along with a local theater owner, we got not only the permit, but also a partnership. We hired professionals to erect the screen, and in the sloped-out cornfield behind it, ramps were bulldozed into stepped parking which accommodated up to one hundred vehicles at a time. Speakers could be draped over half-open car windows.

Business was brisk at both the box office and the concession stand. Because people were looking for an escape from their busy or bored lives, they showed up in droves and in holiday-like humor. Each night just before dusk, cars and trucks lined in a steady procession along the busy highway and then pulled off into our entrance. Before the show started and during intermissions we stayed busy selling Cokes, candy bars and popcorn—lots of popcorn. This was before television. The movies were mostly family-oriented.

The winter months were no different than the summer ones. We often spoke of "playing to a full house." A tractor was kept on standby to pull out cars if they got stuck in the mud or snow. But soon we tired of the whole enterprise. Never having been night people, we didn't enjoy staying up until the wee hours. So, after a couple of seasons, we agreed that this was not the business for us. Luckily, our partner was prepared to buy us out.

We wanted a more theatrical life, but without working in total darkness. We also wanted the freedom of working together. Most of all, we wanted to own our own business.

A couple of times we'd visited an authentic Cherokee Indian village on the Qualla Reservation in North Carolina. It was definitely theater at its most charming, primitive level, with museums, gift shops and Native Americans dressed in elaborate headdresses and fancy buckskins, performing war dances. We wondered aloud if the same kind of production might not work somewhere else.

Trips to the reservation became more frequent. We were suddenly on a mission. Soon we made friends with full-blooded Cherokees Tom and Bettie Lossiah. Tom was a large, square-shouldered man with black, bushy hair and arms that seemed longer than necessary. He stood with pride and possessed a natural dignity. One day he invited us to his home nestled in the Smoky Mountains. We followed his directions until we saw a log cabin sitting on a hill of stacked rocks only a short distance from the road. We parked and began walking up the slope. The cabin was old and weathered, but substantial-looking, with a wood shake roof and a porch flanking one end.

We were welcome. This was no well-mannered disguise, not even in the most remote parts of the Lossiahs' hearts. We could tell they were truly glad we had come.

Inside, the air was heavy with hickory wood smoke curling from a huge, rock fireplace. The front room was large, homey-looking and noticeably clean with scatterings of wood shavings here and there on the floor. On the walls, hung on nails, were strips of basket material.

We had barely sat down when Tom offered us cups of cold water that had just been brought in from the spring. After the hike up the hill from our car, it tasted good. Tom introduced us to his two teenage daughters, Annie and Mary Jane, and then announced, "The Carloftises have come to see our baskets." He showed us several that he and Bettie were working on and then explained the long process which required enormous skill and patience. I was enthralled.

First of all, he told us, he gathered the materials—oak, maple, river cane or honeysuckle vine. If oak or maple was used, he split it into long narrow strips and shaved them down with a very sharp knife, making them smoother and thinner, more pliable and easier to work with. For color, the strips were wound into a loose ball and dropped into a pot of boiling water tinted with natural herb dyes such as yellow root or bloodroot. For a darker, richer appearance, he used the bark from a walnut tree. After the strips soaked for the desired length of time, they were removed from the pot and hung to dry.

A finished basket was a true work of art. I'd read that the Cherokees were considered to be among the most superb Native American weavers, and this proved it. We sat completely riveted by Tom's description and his basket materials in different stages of development—and by Annie's broad smile.

Unlike her sister, who was warm and friendly, Mary Jane was a shy young woman. She lowered her eyes deliberately and turned her head away whenever we spoke to her, but she still seemed conscious of every movement about the room. As she worked, she was clearly competing in expertise with her mother, who was obviously pleased with her daughter's efforts. Indeed, here were two women who were intensely disciplined in their craft.

Looking around, I was suddenly struck by Tom's admiration for Mary's work. He stood and watched her put handles on a finished basket. It was now ready to be taken to one of the downtown stores in Cherokee to be sold. When I told her it was beautiful, she ducked her head, then rose and slipped out of the room. She did not return. I later learned that this kind of modesty was not uncommon among Indian women.

By now Bettie had laid aside the basket she was working on and silently began shaving strips that lay across her apron-covered lap with a pocket knife. Her face was framed with soft lines, and she had expressive, bright eyes.

Bettie had been born on the reservation, we would learn later, and it was her entire world. She knew the Smoky Mountain ranges, and she knew the art of basket making. Her use of colors and her smooth weaving had won her the admiration of natives as well as buyers.

We had already risen to leave when the Lossiahs' two sons walked into the room. Tom and William were both handsome young men who looked to be in their late teens or early twenties. They showed us a stone peace pipe, rubbed to a smooth finish. Their handiwork was incredible. We were amazed. Their father smiled and nodded in approval.

Outside on the porch we admired the mountain peaks' spectacular display of new leaves, a reminder that spring was arriving. Tom was more comfortable with us now, and as he gazed over the landscape he talked of his football days at the Indian school in Oklahoma and of Jim Thorpe. He went on to tell us about "common" food called ramps, which grew wild in the mountains in March and April—and of their healthy benefits after a steady winter diet of meats and dried grains. Ramps tasted like wild onions, he said, but they were much stronger, and they had always been eaten and cherished by the Cherokees. Tom urged us to return soon and eat some ramps with them.

As we headed back down to the car, he strolled along. But about halfway down the middle of the path, he stopped and kicked a walnut-sized rock with the toe of his shoe. Then he bent over and cupped it in his hands as if to conceal it from prying eyes. "There might be gold in this," he declared. Gold had been discovered in Dahlonega, Georgia, thirty years before the California Gold Rush of 1849, and it is still believed by some to lie hidden in the wilds of the Smoky Mountains. That could well have been the event that triggered the blackest episode in the lives of the Cherokees. But according to history, the greatest factor was the ill feeling between the Indians and the frontiersmen.

Prospectors were a daily torment to these helpless people, who were driven in 1838 from their homes over frozen ground and bitterly cold weather 800 miles to Oklahoma. Many walked barefoot and without blankets. Nearly 4,000 died. It came to be called the Trail of Tears.

It was then-President Andrew Jackson, a frontiersman himself, who'd aided and pushed for their removal, even after the Cherokees challenged the state of Georgia, and the case went all the way to the Supreme Court. It was decided in favor of the Cherokees.

But Jackson held firm. "(Chief Justice) John Marshall has made his decision," he insisted. "Now let him enforce it." He disregarded the fact that a great Cherokee, Junaluska, had saved his life at the Battle of Horseshoe Bend in 1814.

Thinking that this might carry some weight with Jackson, Chief John Ross sent Junaluska to beg mercy for his people. But the President turned a deaf ear, saying, "Sir, your audience is ended. There is nothing I can do for you." With those words, the doom of the Cherokee Indians was sealed. Even the ill and elderly were forced out at gunpoint. People were given only moments to collect cherished possessions. Families were separated. White looters followed, ransacking homesteads as the Cherokees were led away.

"People feel bad when they leave Old Nation," related one survivor. "Womens cry and make sad wails, children cry and many men cry...but they say nothing and just put heads down and keep on go towards West. Many days pass, and people die very much."

The few Cherokees who hid out from the federal government continued to struggle on land they could no longer claim until they were aided by Colonel William Thomas, who later became a U.S. Senator and who worked diligently to restore the land to its rightful owners. From there the Qualla Reservation was born.

Since having met the Lossiahs, direct descendants of these courageous people, we were anxious to meet other families as well. So we spent many pleasant hours driving up and down dusty roads, trying to catch glimpses of the Indians in their natural setting. We began making comparative studies of other tribes, and found that unlike the Plains Indians who supported their babies in elaborate beaded cradle boards, the Cherokees used a simple white sheet folded diagonally, criss-crossed in front and tied beneath the baby's bottom in back. This strapped the baby snugly to its mother's warm body, leaving both of her hands free for work. We were impressed.

Our greatest difficulty, we soon realized, would be communicating across cultures. The reservation was primitive compared to the outside world. Men were still using oxen for plowing, and once we saw a man following slowly behind one of these heavy animals. Its horns swung gracefully up and down as it moved along the freshly turned earth. Reluctant to leave, we leaned on a fence and watched. The man never even looked our way. He simply went on with his plowing.

Across the road some children were playing, but when they saw us, they scattered out of sight, flying like small birds to the back of their house. This was not unusual among Native American children, and no wonder; the Trail of Tears, kept alive in everyone's memories, no doubt by their fathers and grandfathers, was enough to justify a permanent fear of strangers.

We watched old women sitting outside their log cabins, crafting beadwork and baskets and firing pottery. It was interesting to learn their different techniques of color and design. They often inscribed the

Cherokee alphabet or animal shapes into their pots. All were different artistic expressions, all lovely and mesmerizing.

So Carlo and I began to formulate a plan. Together we would build a full-scale, detailed replica of a 1700s Indian village as a tourist stop––complete with a living cast. We waved our goodbyes to the Lossiahs and then talked nonstop as we drove back across the mountains, pausing frequently en route to enjoy the scenic views and waterfalls, and to catch an occasional glimpse of a black bear.

We were still up in the air regarding where we should locate. It needed to be an exceptional place, removed from established neighborhoods, yet close to a major highway and near water. There had to be some sense of atmosphere. We could see it in our minds so clearly now—a split-rail fence, teepees with curling smoke and a rustic building with a long welcoming porch stretched across the front. Why not move farther south, perhaps, where the warm season lasted longer and the weather in general was more predictable? We knew that Tom was anxious to leave the reservation, and he would be joined by a friend, another full-blood, William Walkingstick. They were both respected men among their tribe, and they foresaw no delays in recruiting others to join us when the time came. Knowing so little about the Indian culture, it was, of course, an overwhelming, almost inconceivable notion. But we were young and felt equal to the challenge—so why not?

That's when the drama began.

St. Augustine

St. Augustine, Florida, had always held a certain magnetism. We liked the ocean. We were fascinated by the city's history. So one bright day in June, 1954, we loaded our three children into our two-door pea-green Plymouth, strapped their tricycles on top and headed south. We were excited. Mama cried.

We followed the same curving road through the mountains of Tennessee and on through Georgia that we had traveled so many times before. There was little change in scenery, just mile after mile of cotton fields and countryside.

Upon our arrival we spent the first few days as vacationers, swimming and sunning on the beach. We walked along the narrow cobblestone streets, admiring the architecture so heavily influenced by the early Spanish settlers.

There was always a restoration or dig going on somewhere, so we savored each bit of unearthed history. The *coquina* (tile) used in constructing the buildings and walls was a daily fascination, still handsome after all these years. Every day we walked around in our shorts and sunglasses and found new interests, something intriguing to look at. It was a wonderful life.

Early one morning, sitting at breakfast, we saw a sign in the café window that read, "House for rent on Commanche Island, $50.00 a month." At first we thought we had misread it. But no. We decided to check it out and found that the island was just outside the city limits, heading toward Vilano Beach.

Within minutes after leaving the café we crossed a one-way dirt causeway and pulled up in front of a rustic cottage, painted deep, dark green with a screened-in porch wrapping around two sides. Its low-lying roof looked as old as the island itself. Farther on past the cottage stood large, weathered grey two-story clapboard that looked very much at home in its landscape of live oak trees draped in Spanish moss which hung to the ground. It felt eerie and lonely. No way, I thought to myself—but as long as we were there, I figured, I might as well get out and take a look.

I stepped inside the cottage with a cold eye and found two small bedrooms, a kitchen and bath, in addition to the screened-in porch that would eventually become our living room. It was clean, open and airy, furnished sparsely for light housekeeping. Still unmoved, I looked over and spotted with immense relief a television console sitting in one corner with rabbit ears perched on top.

Meanwhile, the children were outside inspecting the sandbox that sat beneath the bedroom window. It was filled with toys, sand buckets, rakes and beach balls. It was the only thing present, in my opinion, that showed any signs of human life. I felt an immediate peace. We rented the place.

The grounds looked like an overgrown jungle, with clumps of cactus and saw brush intertwined with trailing vines and sand. Sand was everywhere, in fact, not to mention the sulfur water. It was terrible. When I bathed the children, they sat in the tub and held their tiny noses. I could only bathe myself with any comfort in water that had been drawn and let set for at least thirty minutes. The fresh air seemed to tone down the sulfur odor.

Our daily activities depended upon the tides. We could only enter or leave the island at low tide. There we were, seven hundred fifty miles away from home and marooned on an island! We saw high drama in that, but somehow I was unable to find the idea very appealing—especially when giant spiders took ownership and had free range of the house. I asked Kit Church, our landlady, if there was anything we could do to get rid of them. "Don't bother them, and they won't bother you," she replied. "Besides, they eat mosquitoes."

Sustained by that thought, I tried not to look when they went spinning from one side of the room to the other right above my head.

Kit owned the island. She was a divorcee living alone with her small daughter, Cathy. Her teenage son was off somewhere at military school. Kit was tall and striking, in her mid-thirties, with short blonde hair. Mornings often caught her out walking the grounds and digging in the oyster beds with a red kerchief tied around her head, knee-high boots and skintight pants. We privately thought that she looked very mysterious and wondered whatever had brought her to this lonely place. But it was peaceful, and Kit was obviously looking for privacy on an island permanently covered with trees, vines and native plants.

We were told that the place was part of her divorce settlement, and that she had earlier owned a beach motel. We tactfully avoided any other discussions about her personal life, but Kit herself told us about the motel and that it had a distinction like no other; when one door closed, the other doors were set ajar from one end of the building to the other. She called it, "The house of slamming doors." Kit, in her new role now, operated a concession stand over on the beach.

Week after week, she wound across the causeway, driving her little white ice cream truck and waving as she passed us, an official celebration that her workday was over. It was good to see a familiar face, and she stopped by frequently to share her thoughts on city politics, business, mosquitoes, where to shop or any other exciting developments that might have occurred locally. She knew the rhythm of the city, and she kept us informed regarding what was hot and what was not.

I was beginning to get homesick and became impatient to return to my family and the Kentucky Mountains. My enthusiasm for Florida was, in fact, waning. It was almost impossible to get comfortable in the intense heat, so we watched a lot of TV, something we didn't have back home. So we spent hours sitting in front of a black-and-white screen that went suddenly silent at midnight, leaving us all alone on an island teeming with wildlife that took full advantage of the darkness.

Early one morning, I heard a ping-ping-ping outside my bedroom window. It was Kit, bending over in the sandbox and digging up an assortment of silverware that Cathy had carried out and buried. Once satisfied that she had found all of the missing pieces, she climbed out of the box and then walked the distance back to her house.

It would be a typical day at the beach for Kit—already crowded by summer tourists and locals alike, carrying picnic baskets and setting up umbrellas and chairs that faced the sun and an outstanding view of the Atlantic Ocean. By 11:00 children were running and playing against waves that flowed back to the sea, a game of volleyball was going on, and a virtual parade of people walked briskly back and forth to the rhythm of the pounding surf. It wasn't noon yet, and the air was already heavy with the smell of Coppertone lotion which bathed scantily clad brown bodies and white bodies, red and blistered from too much sun the day before. Names and funny faces were scrawled at regular intervals in the sand, in addition to elaborate sand castles built by grown-ups, only to be washed away when the tide rolled in. Still, they had managed to recapture a part of their youth before returning to the real world.

One hot afternoon I heard a car come roaring across the causeway at high speed. I rushed outside to investigate. It was Kit—driving a brand-new yellow convertible. The top was rolled back, and Cathy was standing in the front seat beside her. Kit stopped the car and with bubbling excitement exclaimed, "Well, how do you like it?" I replied, "It's beautiful." "I don't know how on earth I'll ever pay for it!" she countered, throwing up her arms. Then she sped away, disappearing into the breeze.

Carlo and I were still searching for our ideal, magical Indian village location. In the meantime we took sightseeing trips to orange groves, walked up and down more cobblestone streets shaded by overhanging balconies, sipped Cokes in restaurants inscribed with "air-conditioned" on their front windows and ate lots of ice cream.

We continually admired the Spanish architecture and landscaping filled with banana trees, bougainvillea, sweet-smelling jasmine and other tropical plants. I had to admit I was developing a serious love affair with beautiful courtyards, as we strolled past one scenic garden and then on to the next. In late afternoon, when it grew cooler, we walked along colorful Mantanzas Bay, looked at the boats and did lots of window shopping.

Carlo's first trip to Florida had taken place back in the late 1930s. He'd liked it then, and he liked it now. In fact, the whole city of St. Augustine fascinated him, especially the Castillo de San Marcos. Perched on the Bay and encircled by a complete water battery, this architectural masterpiece was built in 1695 as a fortress to protect the Spanish from the English settlement. Carlo spent hours retracing the footsteps of the early inhabitants along its many rooms and dark passageways. He was particularly intrigued by the stories of Osceola, the defiant young leader of Seminole resistance. He'd plunged his knife into the treaty he was asked to sign that would move his people from their swamplands in the Southeast to the unoccupied territory west of the Mississippi—and then launched a bloody, seven-year battle against federal troops. Captured and held prisoner at the Castillo by the American government in the

1830s, Osceola was what some called a renegade looking for trouble. Others called him a hero.

Carlo was captivated, and while he sat in silent concentration and dreamed over a cup of hot coffee at the Old Mill across from the fort, the children and I found other things to do. We toured the oldest schoolhouse, walked down the street that was closed to traffic, ate more ice cream and studied new faces. To me the different cultures of people defined the character of the city as much as did its history.

Life in St. Augustine was never short of unusual places, and we were discovering new ones every day tucked away on the back streets, inconspicuous and simple, but well-known to the locals. One such place was Pappy's Seafood House down on Old U.S. 1 Highway. We were told about it by some friends and were anxious to give it a try.

The building was a low, noisy, unpainted structure that had been operated by the same family for decades and was known throughout the area for its simplicity and freshly caught seafood. We arrived early one evening to find it bustling with customers. We were shown to our seats, which were picnic tables and benches, and handed a well-worn menu by a young girl who took our order and left as quickly as she had appeared. We had been to the beach and were famished.

I tucked napkins under the children's chins, and soon our plates arrived, piled high with the catch-of-the-day, shrimp, white fish and crab cakes. All were cooked to perfection—and for less than $3.00. Iced tea was served in fruit jars, something I had never seen before. Everything was oversized at Pappy's, even the proprietor, who sat behind the cash register with her long hair tied in a bun. Hanging on a wall beside her was a sign which boldly stated, "Tourists are not welcome." It was an unforgettable meal. We went back often. Despite staying indoors a lot to escape the heat, we were looking and acting like native Floridians, deeply tanned and familiar with most of the local attractions.

One day as we were driving up San Marcos Avenue, we came across an orange grove that we'd never noticed before. It sat back from the street and was surrounded by a crumbling *coquina* wall. Its day as a fruitful orchard had obviously long passed; now it was overgrown with age and a few twisted orange trees. We could not believe this enchanted treasure was within the city limits, not too small, not too large, ideal in size for what we had in mind—and also, that it was for sale.

The owner was Walter Frasier, a wealthy real estate developer who also owned several attractions in the city. But we knew that we were planning something very different, a village with a living cast of Native Americans. Carlo gave Mr. Frasier a call, and they set up an appointment. Instead of having us meet him at his office, he invited us to come to his home.

We parked our car on the shady side of the street and approached the porch of a lovely Southern-style house that looked out over a deep yard with century-old trees. Inside, the library was elegantly furnished in a traditional European style, with dark, rich woods and red silk wall coverings. Mr. Frasier offered us a warm welcome, and Carlo comfortably extended his hand. I was intimidated. Our little children sat stone-silent.

After he and Carlo had exchanged pleasantries, Mr. Frasier wasted no time getting down to business. He reminded us of the rapid growth of St. Augustine, that it was no longer a haven for wealthy Easterners who spent winters there; families were now flocking to the city and to its beaches year 'round. He seemed a reasonable man, so we told him of our plans to create an outdoor working Indian museum.

We must have been an interesting switch from the daily rounds of people who came to him seeking instant prosperity. Our approach sounded so unusual that he thrust his seat forward and listened intently. Then he leaned back and smiled. Was he as genuinely impressed as he appeared to be—or was he just amused? I couldn't tell. Back and forth the discussion went, until finally Carlo asked, "How much?" Mr. Frasier replied, "$60,000." We thought the price was too high, and we said so. Apparently not wanting to let us go, he inquired, "How about buying half of the grove?" Carlo's answer was, "Let us think it over." Reluctantly we rose, thanked Mr. Frasier for his hospitality and left.

Despite the heat, my homesickness and a hundred other things, we both agreed that the grove was worth every penny of the asking price, and much more. It was also ideal for our plan. But to transform it into a village complete with craftsmen forced us to become a little more realistic—although not much. As usual, we kept an eye out for an alternate location, and as usual, we justified our good intentions by going to the beach, walking around, sightseeing or watching the fishermen at Mantanzas Inlet.

Late one afternoon we were driving back from the Inlet and got stuck in a line of traffic that had pulled to a stop just outside the gates of the Bridge of Lions. There must have been twenty or thirty cars, all barely moving—when in back of us, a car door flew open, and a black man jumped out, waved his huge arms and told us that children had been dropping things from our windows onto the highway for several miles back. We thanked him, turned around and retraced our trip from the Inlet, driving slowly and as close to the shoulder as possible.

At regular intervals along the pavement we found bits of clothing on the ground. A shoe here, a sock there, tops and bottoms—and luckily, my purse that I did not even know was lost. It was a light beige clutch that didn't show up well in the sand. As far as I could make out, we recovered most of the missing articles. Our little children, hot and tired from too many day trips, had been stripping off their clothes and throwing them out of the car window as we drove.

I was beginning to give this whole adventure some serious reconsideration.

By now the sun had gone down, giving us some relief from the heat, and Carlo, showing the first signs of strain, made a great performance of flooring the gas pedal and speeding back to St. Augustine. Over the last weeks I had soaked up plenty of sunshine, walked many historic streets, toured several museums, met dozens of interesting people—and spent countless days of frantic worrying whenever I thought of the poisonous coral snakes, the mountainous anthills, the hideous insects and the smelly sulfur water. What were we doing?

One morning soon afterward I was awakened at daybreak by a tickling sensation. I leaped out of bed, and from the light streaming through my window, I recognized one of our ever-present house guests. A giant spider covered my hand.

We left St. Augustine.

At Fort Sequoyah, Skaggs Trace Historical marker.

The Adventure

*H*aving failed in our Florida venture and happier in the fact that we had, we discussed a foolishly overlooked option. Why not locate right in Kentucky? A new access road had just been built, giving ease to the north-southbound traffic between London and Mt. Vernon. So one day, with nothing else to do, we took a short drive north and crossed the Rockcastle River.

Looking at the ground, colorless and rough, one could easily have decided to move on. But Carlo fixed his practical gaze on the river, with its tall, bordering pine trees. "This would be a good place for business," he said. "Long views from both directions and plenty room for parking!"

He began making inquiries and found that the locals had always assumed the acreage was part of the Daniel Boone National Forest. We had to find out for sure.

One afternoon, following several trips back and forth to the river, Carlo saw an old man walking in slow motion with a stick and his coat slung over one shoulder. He stopped the car and struck up a conversation. Walter Kemper, he discovered, knew the property well and seemed to be an authority on all adjoining tracts. This particular strip, Walter said, belonged to Bill and Ollie Emily—thirty acres or more, surrounded by the National Forest and bounded by the Rockcastle River. Walter had spent his life here and was a friend of the Emilys, truck farmers living in Reading, Ohio.

We wasted no time in contacting them. Not wishing to sound too eager, we merely asked if they were interested in selling their property. They hedged. After a decent interval, we phoned again. And again. Several months and several calls later, they finally invited us to visit them.

The farm sat back from the main road on seventy-five rich acres that produced corn and hay. It was also a range for beef cattle. Their house was a late nineteenth-century two-story brick that looked very much at home in the old farming community. I was charmed by it, and by all of the outbuildings that made up the landscape. We enjoyed a pleasant visit and met their two sons—but nothing was settled regarding the property.

Finally Carlo offered what we thought was a fair price: $4000. When the Emilys accepted, words could not express our relief. Somewhat to our surprise, our search for a site was finally over.

On the same day the deed was signed, we walked down to the river to celebrate our purchase and sat beneath the tall trees on a thick carpet of pine needles. It had been a wonderful afternoon. Rockcastle River was just below us, the trees' shadows were lengthening on the ground, and we thought there could be no better place in the world than this to start our business. As a boy Carlo had swum often in the Cumberland River. I'd been born on Little Goose Creek and waded in it as a child, looking for minnows and tadpoles, with only the gurgling sounds for company. Strangely out of place? No, not to us. We were home.

Although there was no plumbing or electricity on the property, we were ready to start building. The fresh smell of spring sharpened our senses. We found two local carpenters who seemed eager to take on the job. Albert Radford was a short, portly man who wore loose-fitting overalls and a matching washed-out billed cap that sat flat on his round, bald head. He talked with a Tampa cigar between his teeth, rolled his big eyes and was fully prepared to wait patiently through any delays that might occur from time to time. He traced local ancestry and told many stories.

Albert knew a lot of things about a lot of things, and due to his years of experience, he could handle the most unexpected details with ease. He propped up an old Model-T Ford engine on concrete blocks for electrical power. His son-in-law, Jimmy Eversole, small and lean, came to work each day in pressed khakis. They made an ideal team. One measured, one sawed—and together their work went exactly according to schedule.

They first built a large, one-room structure that was to be our on-site living quarters. It was open and airy, with no inside walls, just windows––lots of windows. Constructed in only five days, the design suited us fine. After all, it would soon be summer. We worked all day, and then with only a kerosene lantern for light, we went to bed at nightfall with the stars shining through the cracks of the rough siding. We had cracks in our floors too. Yet truthfully, it was a good life. We found romantic flavor in the fact that we were realizing a dream—a wild dream that we didn't know a whole lot about.

One morning, as Carlo was making coffee on our one-burner kerosene stove, he spilled some grounds on the floor. He stopped and made a great display of cleaning up the mess by merely raking the coffee grains through the cracks with his shoe. He grinned. This was fun for now. But we both admitted that we needed to do something soon.

Both of our families had already made it clear that they thought we had lost our minds. In fact, they hadn't hesitated to say so. They worried about economics. My main concerns were the bugs and rattlesnakes.

Over the next three months, the valley was inhabited by frenzied workmen, zipping across the landscape, wiring buildings, drilling wells, cutting trails and planting shrubs and flowers native to the area. They knew we were in a hurry. Warm weather wouldn't last forever.

We traded our car for a two-ton truck, and I became the official driver. There was no one to watch the children, so I piled them into the truck's cab and drove down U.S. 25 to lumber mills, block and gravel quarries—and once, intent on purchasing some inexpensive wood, over a bumpy field through a cow pasture. When we stopped to open and close the gates behind us, the children's wide eyes darted back and forth, looking out for crazed cows. Even I was relieved when we got back to the main road. We rewarded ourselves by stopping for chocolate pie before heading home.

One day I returned with materials, and before I could cut off the truck's motor, I saw a brand-new cash register resting on planks between two sawhorses. Carlo! The walls of the store weren't even up yet. I was taken aback, yet utterly charmed by his optimism.

The children were finding so much to be delighted about. They discovered nature, wide-awake and stirring, with ants, worms, rabbits, squirrels and a wide variety of birds. They picked wildflowers, made hats, belts and umbrellas from the tulip tree that stood beside our front door. They swung on grapevines and played in the sawdust piles. They were getting plenty of open air and exercise and were so happy that I could hardly get them to come inside long enough to eat. Their frolicking freedom was similar to what I had once enjoyed on Little Goose Creek. When night came, they fell instantly asleep.

When I could finally lie down, a stillness brooded in the woods, and an odd sense of isolation crept over me. But I was so tired from the day's activities that I soon fell fast asleep to the sounds of croaking bullfrogs and the lonesome call of the whippoorwill. My mind was as free as the river that flowed past me.

Located directly across from the Indian village was Sand Hill. The ridge ran several miles north to south over hills and slopes that fell toward the river. In some places the sandstone rocks flowed from rich pinks to warm yellows and browns. The foliage was beautiful. Many times I went there to see the red buds and dogwoods that bloomed profusely in the spring. Fall would be equally lovely, with its palette of color extending down to the river and on into Livingston—an old, undeveloped settlement where our workmen lived. Many of them and their fathers before them had been born there.

By June, 1955, the store was finished. We were ready to stock it with Native American handcrafted merchandise. The porch running across the front gave it a warm, pioneer look—ideal, we thought, for our woodland setting. Loads and loads of rhododendrons and ferns were wheel barrowed in and planted along the meandering paths that led to footbridges and down wooded slopes.

We had the July and August vacationers to look forward to. School was out for the summer, and northern families would be heading to the mountains or even farther south to the beaches. We'd been told that October was the month that grandmothers began to travel. They were great shoppers, relishing fewer crowds and cooler temperatures. November and January would bring Canadians rushing to our borders in search of warmer weather. We were ready.

I surveyed—not our tables, sparsely furnished with merchandise—but the view behind the counter. It was a blank wall in dire need of decorating. But with what? I gathered up the children and sped to Renfro Valley to seek out its founder, John Lair. John was an entrepreneur who had spearheaded a country music radio show which broadcast live for years. After I'd explained briefly why I had come, he escorted me into his office and began removing artifacts from his walls, then carried them outside and loaded them into my trunk. He made no mention of when he'd expect their return.

In time, others would help us as well. Clell Pike arranged for load after load of fresh dirt to be dumped on our property, thus enabling

Carlo Carloftis and his dad, George Karloftis.

Carlo Carloftis in his 20s.

Myrtle Rhodes Karloftis, Carlo's mother.

Carlo Carloftis, U.S. Army Air Corps during World War II.

The Hub Grill in downtown Pineville, Kentucky.

Carlo and Lucille Carloftis during the early years of marriage.

Above: Lucille Carloftis' mother, Verda Marcum.

Left: Lucille's father, Robert Franklin Bowling.

Lucille Carloftis with Koula and Betsy in Florida.

Carlo Carloftis with Buzz, Carcille and Koula.

Flaming Arrow with Koula, Buzz and Carcille.

Betsy and Koula with a visitor to the store.

Buzz, Koula, Carcille and Betsy inside old shop.

Tennessee Ernie Ford with Betsy and Koula.

Koula, Betsy (holding Jon) and Dusty.

Dinah George (holding Betsy), Bettie Lossiah with Koula, and Julius George with Buzz.

Jon in Indian made basket and Dusty.

Lightfoot and Dusty.

Lone Fox, Carlo, John F. Stahl and Chief.

Lucille's grandmother, Margaret Garrison.

Ruby LeFevers, behind counter in the store.

First store, Fort Sequoyah, 1955 or 1956.

Surrey ride at Fort Sequoyah, Indian and Riverboat Town.

Lightfoot and Jon.

The Palace in Riverboat Town.

Street scene in Riverboat Town.

William Walkingstick and a basket maket at Ft. Sequoyah old village.

Tom Lossiah, Lightfoot, in a scene from the drama McNitts Defeat at Levi Jackson State Park.

Buzz with one of the stray dogs, B.J.

Street scenes from Fort Sequoyah Indian Village and Riverboat Town.

The interior of the old store

us to build and grow. John Carpenter of the London Bucket gave us time to pay for our much-needed materials. David McCauly helped us to navigate through state board regulations. Mary Evelyn Leach, Bible school teacher and mother of three, spent many hours in her kitchen, cooking and sharing. She had an open door policy regarding other people's children. Mine would visit often.

The day finally came for our grand opening. At sundown the night before, William Walkingstick arrived from Cherokee with the eight-member Indian cast he had promised. But the word had spread more widely than anticipated. Our small house quickly became overflow quarters. Late that night, when I pushed open our seldom locked door, I was stunned to find all of the beds filled with sleeping Indians. On the screened-in porch our children were folded up like pillows on the sofa, all sound asleep. There was no room for me anywhere. I dropped into a chair and waited for daylight.

As I closed my eyes, I tried to visualize the business we were starting as successful—but all I could think of was the lovely house we'd left behind in Pineville with its balconies, spacious beamed rooms, polished mahogany and Italian chandeliers. Sitting there, wide awake, I began feeling doubts rising in my mind like murky water. Our money was nearly gone, and we still had an Indian cast to pay. What had we done? Too late now. The stage was set, the players were here, and we were waiting for our audience.

Opening day was a nightmare. Despite the heavy traffic, few travelers stopped, and then it seemed to be mostly out of curiosity. At the end of a very long day, we closed our doors and counted our money. The store's take was less than $10.00.

We swallowed our disappointment, collapsed in bed and waited for morning. The harsh warnings of our families rang louder in our ears. Yet Carlo still believed that our venture would work. I liked his vision. By now we had no choice. Days passed.

The following week, the Mt. Vernon *Signal* sent reporter Georgia Clark Harmon to write a story about the county's newest business. William Walkingstick gave her a tour of the village, and as they strolled together along the wooded paths, she saw artisans at work in their native costumes. Unnatural as it must have seemed for her to observe real live Indians in Kentucky, she caught the drama and wrote a fascinating story, which was published along with photographs and which spread the news across the entire state of Kentucky and throughout southern Indiana. The very day that it appeared in the Louisville *Courier Journal,* our parking lot was filled.

Visitors congregated under shaded canopies at the Ceremonial Ground. Tom Lossiah demonstrated the art of the blowgun. He described how his ancestors had hollowed out cane and shaped darts from sticks and thistle. Then he pressed both hands to his mouth, took a deep breath—and plop, the arrow shot from the blowgun and hit the center of his target. Everyone was awed. This curious weapon, he explained, was typically used for small game and had an accuracy of up to sixty feet. But the bore had to be smooth, the thistle thick enough to fill the bore, and the blow had to be quick through the tube. Our children, who stayed down in the village a great deal, eventually became quite skilled in the art.

The bead maker sat a few steps away at the door of a one-room cabin with a bark roof. She made bright, delicate jewelry by stringing multicolored beads with a simple needle and thread. For headbands, belts and cuffs she used a loom.

The Sweat House, a fixture in every Indian village, was partly underground, with a small opening made of logs. Inside were the fire pit and pole beds. In the old days, once or twice a week, men, women, and children took turns steaming themselves free of ailments by pouring water over hot rocks. When the heat became unbearable, they went outside for a dip in the creek, and during the winter months, they tumbled naked in the snow. They believed that this cleansed and purified their bodies.

The animal trap sat at a low point near the river. The path followed across a foot bridge to a log cabin with a rock chimney and shake roof. Pole beds were hung from the walls and padded with dried leaves. This was where the basket weavers sat. Bettie Lossiah, known as the Basket Maker, fully deserved her title. The baskets were elegant and handsomely designed. They were woven into different shapes and sizes; some could even be lined and carried as purses. A few were tiny enough for trinkets. One was a cylinder with rings on each side that were fashioned like the large loop earrings that I wore. When I later saw them in stores on the reservation, I thought that I had probably inspired the look.

The centerpiece of the village was the Council House, a seven-sided structure built with clay and mud and representing the seven clans of the Cherokee Nation. Visitors seated themselves around a central fire pit and a symbol illustrating an ancient belief that when all the fires were put out and the ashes cleaned, a new year had begun. This gala event was called the Fire Festival. The Council House fire was sacred. From it, all other fires from the seven clans were relighted so that they could benefit from its magical powers.

Clad in authentic Cherokee costumes, William Walkingstick and Sam Greywolf stood near the Council fire and told the story of the Trail of Tears to a captivated audience. Both were eloquent speakers, with dramatic yet soft voices and undeniable charm. Clearly, they were establishing positive relations between the Native
Americans and our visitors.

The Indians would name our village Fort Sequoyah in honor of the Chief who was probably the greatest of all Cherokees. He had single-handedly created a written alphabet for his people without being able to read or write any other language. Except for the sound of the letter 'm' the complete alphabet could be spoken without closing the lips. By the 1820s, Sequoyah's syllables brought literacy and a formal governing system with a written constitution. He is still renowned to this day for having advised the Cherokees to follow a path of wisdom and tolerance.

By now we felt we were ready for anything—almost. But in the beginning, it wasn't easy to work with the Indians. Many seemed shy, even withdrawn, and although they understood and spoke perfect English, they chose to communicate only in their native tongue, which by no means encouraged conversation. They also had a marked distaste for anything resembling regimentation, so repeat performances put a real strain on their valued independence. I grudgingly admired this quality— —until early one morning when we opened the store and discovered that there was no one down in the village. They were all gone.

It was difficult to explain to customers who arrived that day expecting a guided tour. Somehow I offered one feeble excuse after another. People continued to browse and shop, most in pleasant humor.

The following morning, the Indians returned. They appeared in the village as usual in their long, patterned skirts and buckskins and began weaving and carving to the soft beat of a rawhide tom-tom. Their eyes were lowered. They said nothing.

Noon came, and then late afternoon. Finally, when Jimmy Screamer strolled into the store I asked for an explanation. He shrugged. Everyone had gotten so homesick for Cherokee, he said, and that they simply had to leave. I was stunned. "But why," I protested, "did they go at night?"

Jimmy paused at the door, lifted his chin and replied in a deep voice, "its cooler that way."

Before I could say anything else, he was at the end of the porch and heading back down toward the village.

Chief R. Deerfoot

*I*ndians from other tribes began arriving. The first was an Oklahoma Cherokee by the name of Chief R Deerfoot, who was an evangelist and an herbalist. He and Carlo had met earlier on the reservation, and because Deerfoot was searching for a location to house his artifact collection, they had discussed the possibility of opening a museum here at the village. After all, our business was already built around the Indian theme, and a museum would be an interesting added attraction. We knew of no other one in Kentucky that was totally devoted to the American Indian.

First, however, we needed to construct another building. Like everything else our carpenters had built, it was soon finished—a simple, windowless structure shaped like an oversized box. Only its low roofing gave it some measure of character. From the highway it looked as if someone had started assembling and then lost interest. Yet its rustic appearance looked natural in our wooded setting. Ever the optimist, Carlo considered the pleasant possibility that if this particular venture did not work out, the building could easily be converted into something else useful. But we hoped it would meet with Deerfoot's approval. We had no written contract regarding how long he would stay.

Early one morning, as the fog lifted from the valley and dissolved over the landscape, a car with a trailer hitched behind it pulled up in the parking lot. The engine stopped, and the driver emerged, accompanied by a big brown-and-white curly St. Bernard dog.

Deerfoot was a large man, tall and muscular, with snow-white hair and skin that was deeply and evenly tanned. At first I thought I detected an air of arrogance about him, but when he spoke, his voice was tender and kind. He silently wandered around with his dog and seemed to be regarding the place as an interesting challenge. The ground was flat, some of it sheltered by tall trees and some covered in gravel. It was obvious that we were expecting lots of business, because there were plenty of parking spaces. We hoped that Deerfoot took that as an encouraging sign.

Within less than a week, with the help of other Indians, the museum was ready to open. Inside the front door was a maze of wire that directed visitors past walls covered with newspaper clippings and photographs. The heat hung heavy as they strolled through colorful displays of rugs, saddle blankets, pottery, tomahawks, peace pipes of all shapes and designs, drums, buckskins, beaded moccasins and elaborate eagle feather headdresses that had been worn by prominent chiefs and warriors. A hand-lettered sign described each artifact.

Deerfoot sat in a rocking chair outside the entrance and pocketed the admission charge, not saying much. And when the evening sun dropped behind the hills, he closed the front door, got into his car, and with his big dog sitting on the seat beside him, he took a leisurely drive down the river to Livingston to buy a newspaper and some groceries before returning to his tiny apartment behind the museum.

Deerfoot's Caucasian wife, Sally, worked in Cincinnati as a secretary and joined him only on the weekends, apparently pleased with the chance to escape into the country. Petite and much younger than he, she had classic bone structure, and her dark hair was held back in a soft bun by two striking pins. Unlike the rest of us in our sunny clothes and turquoise jewelry, Sally dressed conservatively in high-necked blouses with long, close-fitting sleeves, skirts which fell to mid-calf and plain, low-heeled pumps. I saw no jewelry other than a thin gold wedding band.

She came into the store, polite and complimentary. I showed her around, introducing her to the variety of merchandise that we sold. She didn't stay long.

As the season wore on, she would stop by to see if we had stocked anything new or just to talk. I looked forward to her short visits and found that we both had an avid interest in herbs. We sold a limited packaged supply in the store, and we discussed their medicinal value. Sally seemed to have a wide knowledge regarding the subject.

But every time, our conversation inevitably traveled back to Deerfoot, whom she affectionately called "Doctor." I was impressed with the deep love and respect, despite their curious age difference, which she showed him.

Deerfoot was born in the Tallaquah Indian Territory in Oklahoma in 1871. At age twelve he took the Indian test of manhood, and at sixteen he took what they referred to as the Chieftan's test. In those days it was customary for Cherokees to give their children only an initial at birth––revealed in a name when the child reached age ten. But before his tenth birthday Deerfoot's mother died, leaving him the eternal mystery of never knowing his full name.

His mother spoke no English, but she knew both the pitfalls and advantages of the white man's ways from the missionaries who had visited their reservation. When she realized she was dying, she called Deerfoot to her. "Son," she said, "Mother is going to the Happy Hunting Grounds. The Great Spirit is waiting, your father is there, and I must go too. Will you promise me a few things? Promise to get a paleface education. Never get put behind prison bars. Realize and worship the Great Spirit—and always remember." Those were her last words.

The story that Deerfoot laid out downplayed the early life of a boy whose father was killed in a fight between the Creeks and the Cherokees over a livestock watering hole. But the force that gave momentum to his narrative was the episodic, uncivilized life he led until he was seventeen years old, and later, of his considerable personal accomplishments.

In 1889, when Deerfoot turned eighteen, he was instructed by an Indian agent to leave the reservation and attend the Indian School in Carlisle, Pennsylvania. At first he refused to go, but after intense persuasion from both the agent and his best friend, Lightfoot, he agreed.

"I had never seen a house," Deerfoot related, "nor a horse and buggy—although I had seen horses without buggies. I had never seen a railroad train nor a window glass or a bed, and had never tried to eat any civilized food. After we had traveled for two suns and one sleep, we came to the depot. Now, imagine how I felt when I first saw that building. I just stood there staring at it, afraid that it was going to fall over on me. I hadn't noticed that I was standing on a manmade platform. I gave a war-whoop and jumped, right about the time the big black engine blew its whistle. I started running and hit a buggy. After getting untangled from the buggy, I saw some trees. I knew they couldn't hurt me, so I made my way toward them. Well, finally I managed to board the train."

His first few days at Carlisle were intensely frightening. He was afraid of being trapped between gates, so he jumped over fences. Once he walked right through a screen door. He had difficulty going up and down steps. For the first time in his life, he slept in a bed between sheets and saw his own reflection in a mirror. The food, he said, was the hardest adjustment of all.

On his way to school one morning, he passed a store where the door was open. He saw some meat hanging from a hook above the counter. He went inside, tore off a slice and snatched some potatoes and onions. He sat down on the floor and ate, then rose and continued on his way.

Yet somehow, even with new customs and a foreign language to learn, Deerfoot eventually established himself on campus through his wit, his intellect and his willingness to learn. After four years at Carlisle, he was ready to explore life further outside his own culture. He traveled to Canada.

One night in Manitoba, he sat drunk on a curbstone with a blonde on one arm and a brunette on the other, listening halfheartedly to a street corner evangelist. Deerfoot instantly recognized the song the man began singing, "There's Not a Friend Like the Lowly Jesus," because he had heard his mother sing it in their native tongue.

He slowly rose from where he was sitting and pulled the Indian teachings that he carried with him from his wampum belt. Then he walked up to the preacher and asked him to show him what he was talking about.

They compared scriptures. The preacher said, "Stranger, it is the word of God." Amazed to see the connection between his belief in the Great Spirit with that of Christianity, the conviction of faith washed over him. Some friends appeared and declared, "Oh, look. Chief has become sober at last."

He was baptized into the Christian faith, and in the spring of 1899, preached his first sermon, which led seventeen other people to Christ. From that day on, Deerfoot spoke in every state and in some foreign countries. The central theme of his talks combined the life of an evangelist with that of a Cherokee Indian.

Wherever he went, he was well-received, and his lectures were very popular. In Berlin, Germany, he spoke to an audience of over a thousand people. In London, England, he spoke in the halls of Westminster Abbey and was eventually heard by King George V and Queen Mary.

But his most thrilling adventure took place in China in 1902 during the Boxer Rebellion. As he stood in the street preaching the Gospel, a group of hungry headsmen arrived, looking for blood and trouble. The young missionary woman sent to lead the singing was overwhelmed with fear and anxiety. "Don't worry," Deerfoot reassured her. "Jesus is with us. They can't kill us but once. We must fear only he who can kill both soul and body." But by the end of the service, those same headsmen were proclaiming testaments of peace and brotherly love. "I've had the two highest callings," Deerfoot concluded, "excepting none. I became an herbalist for the healing of bodies and a preacher for the healing of souls."

Deerfoot was an exceptional man, a world traveler, a lecturer and an ardent believer in God. He also played an important role on the stage that we were trying to create. His artifact collection added an intriguing dimension. Unfortunately, his time with us was much too short. He suffered from a heart ailment and had to leave. He and Sally moved to Cincinnati, where he later died. Sally continued to visit us from time to time, and for a while we exchanged postcards, but eventually, as with so many others we have known, we lost all contact with her.

The Front Door.

The American Spirit Is All Around

Construction was completed. Dogwood trees were now in full blossom, and the mountains were scattered with red buds bordered by tall pines in magnificent shades of green. A split-rail fence provided the perfect backdrop for the large canvas teepee that sat beside our store. It carried an intended aura, rustic and inviting. The highway was always busy with traffic, and we were beginning to establish a fine, prosperous business.

But there were so many obstacles to overcome, so much to learn. Nothing was easy, whether it was distributing advertising brochures to area motel desk clerks or arranging for ongoing media coverage. But the greatest problem, we came to realize, was that we didn't have enough water to furnish both our home and our business. We had dug five wells, and still there was a shortage.

Many nights after we had closed the store, we primed the pump by slowly pouring water into it to create a suction, which pulled the water upward. Sometimes it took hours and several tries to succeed, and then the water could still be completely lost overnight.

When this occurred, I lined up the children in the bathroom early in the morning before they left for school and washed the "sleepy" from their eyes with a washcloth that I dipped into the holding tank behind the commode. One day I decided I'd give myself a leisurely shampoo. I lathered my hair and then massaged it, taking my time. But when I was ready to rinse, the unthinkable happened. The well had once again gone completely dry. I had to call and call for someone to prime the pump—and then wait patiently with soapy hair before the water began flowing again.

Stories like that would eventually become interesting family tales of survival—as would the one about Carcille minding the store. Sometimes, when business was slow, Carlo and I would walk back to the house to refill our coffee cups. We left Carcille in charge, instructing her to call out the back door if any customers showed up. At age six, she was delighted to play shopkeeper.

One day, when we didn't hear from her, we just sat at the kitchen table and lingered over our coffee. Minutes went by. Finally we headed back to the store. To our astonishment, there were several people walking around—but there was no sign of Carcille. One older couple approached us and remarked,"The cutest little girl was sitting here on a stool, and she welcomed us with, 'Make yourselves at home.' Then she hopped off the stool, left through the back door, and we never saw her again." I tried to explain, but they smiled and waved my words away. "We knew someone would come eventually," they said. "We waited, because we felt right responsible."

For all practical purposes, I did the shopping and banking. Carlo felt he was better behind the counter. I always took the children with me. One day I drove to the bank to make a deposit. This was long before the convenience of drive-throughs. By then we owned a station wagon, and the children could sit in three different places. No restraining belts back then, and no infant carriers.

Once on the main road heading home, I turned around and discovered that baby Dusty was missing. Horrified, I realized I had forgotten him in the bank. I turned the car around and sped back into town. Sure enough, there he sat in president Smock's lap, picking on the typewriter and eating ice cream.

I didn't know what to say or how to say it. I was too ashamed and embarrassed. But back in the car, I looked at my healthy and happy children and thought to myself, life may be hectic, but it's also beautiful.

Locals at first greeted us with enormous curiosity, but when school started in September, we began building relationships with the teachers and some of the other parents. We bought everything in town that we could, our groceries, clothing, hardware—and we ate at local restaurants. Our children were making friends, and we were beginning to feel at home, although the Indian village was becoming more and more our world.

Still, we attended all of the school functions. I remember going to Band Day where 5,000 students assembled each year at the Eastern Kentucky University football field. It was cold and snowy. We mothers sat on the bleachers and shivered. Jo Webb reached over and asked to borrow my binoculars. When she handed them back to me she remarked, "Just as I expected. Everyone's out of step except Buzz and Bobby."

At the end of a busy workday, the children and I often took a drive down Skaggs Creek to buy eggs and cutup chickens at the Blackburn Farm. Josie Blackburn placed the chicken pieces in a covered bucket and then lowered it into a spring of running water to keep cool until I could get there. They had no electricity yet down their way.

Her husband Joe was a wiry old man with a fine manner and a deep, chuckling voice. He wore a shirt buttoned to the collar, a suit coat, black shoes and a felt hat as dark as midnight. Looking at him sitting with his legs crossed, holding his walking stick, I was reminded of a Norman Rockwell painting.

Their farm lay in a handsome setting of cleared bottom land along the river. And in the center on a rise stood their two-story house, made from large, hand-hewn logs dating back to the late 1700s. In the early days it had been an inn for overnight travelers. I often wondered how many families it had given shelter. The surroundings had not changed much. I was fascinated by the beauty and history of this old structure that seemed so far away from the outside world, yet very much a part of it.

On summer evenings the Blackburn family gathered outside around a long, wooden table and ate their supper of fresh, garden-grown vegetables. Grandchildren were always present, laughing and playing, far from the noise of highway traffic. I always enjoyed my visits there and studied the field in its solitude.

Five miles down the road was our town, Livingston; a hamlet, really. Its commerce and school depended upon the outlying rural districts and travelers along U.S. 25. At the turn of the century, Livingston was a flourishing railroad center with a bank and several small hotels, but when the roundhouse moved, the town went into a steady business decline. Still, it remained alive with movement and was a good place to live.

There were four churches and a collection of neat white one- and two-story houses with porch swings and climbing rose vines. Hedges and colorful flower gardens bordered these pretty, modest Main Street homes.

The heartbeat of the town was the school, graded 1-12, that sat right on the edge of the street. We were impressed with this facility and its dedicated teachers. The gym had once held the funeral of Dr. R.G. Webb, the town's only physician, who died sometime in his eighties and whose passing was marked by an overflowing crowd of people.

One of the town's chief citizens was Foster Mullins. He operated a grocery store on the corner and was devoted to the Christian Church. For a short time when he was in the hospital, he begged to be released so that he could attend Sunday church services. Unable to sit up, he reclined on the front pew until the service was over. He held an international record for attendance at the Masonic Lodge, a life verified beyond any shadow of doubt to commitment and Christian faith.

His store was comfortable and nostalgic, with pressed tin ceilings, old counters and showcases, and a brass cash register with a brass credit slip holder. You could always count on a warm welcome as he assisted everyone with grocery lists by retrieving items himself from the white painted shelves, taking every opportunity to be as agreeable as possible. I never saw him angry or upset, although he was mildly critical of parking meters and instant mashed potatoes. He even made home deliveries. Children hopped into the back of his pickup truck and went along for the ride. On Sunday mornings he and another esteemed citizen, Charlie Mounts, went to nearby homes and ferried the children to Sunday school and church.

His house was known for its red shutters, red porch swing and chairs and an explosion of red salvia that lined the walkway. His kind and gentle wife, Mabel, loved red, and she shared her passion with all who passed by. Both were clearly revered by the citizens of Livingston. She lived well into her eighties, and he died at the age of 99.

There were others, plenty of others who were held in high regard, who went about their daily lives with pride and in their own way. Nothing was hurried. We saw people crossing the street to Halcomb's Sundry for their morning newspapers, stopping at the post office, sitting on the corner whittling or moving around in the P.L. Poynter store, a late nineteenth-century two-story clapboard that sat on the south end of town with windows that boldly proclaimed *Groceries, hardware and paint.* Once inside you could find just about anything you needed to carry on the simplest way of living.

The C.H. Webb store was the only place in town where residents could receive a haircut from the proprietor himself, while shopping for groceries, dry goods or wearing apparel. He also sold furniture and kitchen appliances. I can still see the beautiful packages that his wife Jo hand-wrapped. They had a soft, elegant look that was so recognizable at birthdays, weddings and showers that they could have easily been stamped with the letter J.

But it was the Mullins store at the north end of town which tended to reflect the character of the community. Men spent hours sitting on front benches, where their speech competed with the noises of the big diesel trucks across the street at the Livingston Motor Company and the laughter and off-key whistling of Archie Bales. This was where the Indians traded, and like all other stores in town, it had the distinct atmosphere and flavor of a late nineteenth-century establishment.

The town's hot spot was the bustling Bingham's Café. That's where the young people hung out during school lunch breaks and before and after ball games, eating hamburgers, hot dogs, drinking Cokes and listening to their favorite recordings on the jukebox. Courtships formed among the young boys and girls. And as the sun shone through the huge plate glass window, they were certain that this happy time of their lives would go on forever.

Just around the bend outside of Livingston, perched right on the edge of the Rockcastle River was the Trolley Inn, an actual trolley car that had been remodeled into a 1950s-style diner. Thanks to proprietor Ruth Eversole, it had an instant charm, a comfortable, happy atmosphere. Stepping inside, you walked directly into a counter that ran the full length of the diner. And you could play your personal jukebox selections without leaving your barstool. The favorites of the day were "Great Balls of Fire" and "Boll Weevil Sitting on a Bale of Hay."

The diner was low and noisy, and it smelled delicious. The blend of fresh-brewed coffee, beef stew, frying hamburgers, and the sweet aroma of home-baked pies and cobblers were a gentle reminder that food, plain and simple, can be so good.

We ate there often.

Social activities were conducted by the Lion's Club, Masonic and Eastern Star, the churches and the school. Birthdays and weddings were huge events—but it was the school that really brought everyone together.

Citizens worked hard. There were no swimming pools, second homes or long winter trips south. If anyone did venture away from home, it was only for a short time. People stood on the sidewalks and talked or sat on their front porches and watched the north-south bound traffic go by, apparently content right where they were.

That was more than forty years ago. Today, of course, the town has changed. The school where hallways once rang with the laughter of children is no longer there. Part of it is now a community center. The civic clubs are gone too, as well as some of the old buildings. But it's still a destination, a retreat, and it's not uncommon on the weekends to see the streets lined on both sides of the highway with parked cars.

Each year during the Homecoming, there's standing room only. People of all ages come from far and near to visit family and friends, to enjoy the Old Timer's Ball Game, to listen to the local talent play music and to sample good food. Maude Mullins, instrumental in starting the Homecoming, leads the singing at the Baptist church with a voice that's still strong and clear at age 92. Pauline Poynter of Poynter's Hardware serves as secretary.

What is it about Livingston and that unique spirit of small-town America? There are indeed thousands of those towns where people remain for a lifetime—because they're happy, they're comfortable, and they know they already have everything they could possibly want.

Diversity Among
The Indians

*A*ll at once, it seemed, the population at the village increased dramatically. Native Americans, some of whom were fine artists themselves, began coming to visit family and friends. Indians from other tribes showed up as well. Some just passed through, some stayed a week or so, while others stayed for the entire season.

Even the least talented among them were treated like celebrities. Their presence created an entertaining atmosphere. Many visitors had never seen an Indian in real life. There was so much energy here; our place on the river had turned into a comfortable little corner of the world. And we looked forward to each day as we dressed in our costumes of turquoise jewelry and beaded deerskin moccasins.

We sold our merchandise so quickly that trips to the reservation to replenish our stock became more and more frequent. This was before the interstate system, so it was a long, tiresome drive. We also went deep into the mountains and bought baskets and pottery from Indian families. For fast deliveries, such as our Indian dolls from Asheville, we depended upon the always reliable Greyhound bus. When Irene Johnson from Corbin sent a pound cake to Dusty, she had it delivered by Greyhound.

Once when we approached Cherokee, Koula was sitting with one of the Indian girls who was riding along. When she realized where we were, Koula began jumping up and down, saying, "I want to see an Indian! I want to see an Indian!" The young girl laughed and said, "Who do you think is holding you?"

Henry Reid and his wife, both Cherokees from the reservation, were among our original cast. He was a carver, and she made beadwork. Henderson Welch was another—big, fat and funny, with a personality that matched his size. I would ask, "How are you today?" He would pat his tummy with both hands and reply, "Eiga, eiga." He loved food and talked about it often.

Julius Wilnoty was a skilled Cherokee craftsman. He chipped arrowheads from pieces of flint, charming his audiences. His wife Nancy worked down in the village. Others contributed to the colorful history of Fort Sequoyah, and each marched to a different drum.

It had never occurred to us that the village would attract so many diverse Indian families. Elizabeth Hill and her daughter Peggy were also among the original cast. Elizabeth made beautiful beadwork. Geraldine Jackson made pottery. Our clay was not suitable—too much sand, she said. When she tried to fire it, it crumbled. So Mrs. Bigmeat, back on the reservation, made it for us.

Before the end of the summer, we had caught the attention of Gray Wolf, a Cayuga-Delaware descendent. He was born into the Wolf clan near Miami, Oklahoma. He had served in the infantry and paratroopers for four years during World War II and was decorated three times. His wife was a pretty Shawnee named Maxine Blue Jacket. They were a charming and handsome couple, and we were delighted that they had joined us.

Gray Wolf brought not only his talent, but an interesting history of his Great Iroquois Nation ancestry. Before 1750, a group of Cayuga, Seneca, Mohawk and others broke away and migrated into Pennsylvania, then on into Ohio. They were called Mingeive or "Mingo," meaning "treacherous" in Algonquin. And when the white people began moving into the Ohio country, they found the name fitting, because the Mingos fought them bitterly to save their homes and land.

The Mingos took part in every battle that was fought in the Old Northwest Territory. And after the treaty of Greensville, Ohio, Gray Wolf's tribe was given land in the North Central part, along with the Wyandottes, who were their allies. They began calling the Mingos the Senecas of Sandusky, because some of their chiefs were Senecas.

Gray Wolf's people had become farmers, and like their white neighbors, they built a school and a church. But the U.S. government didn't want Indians in Ohio, and the white farmers wanted their land, so they were removed into Kansas, then into Oklahoma. When the Civil War began, they were Northern sympathizers and were moved back to Kansas. When the war was over, they lost their land and had to start all over. This time they moved to Oklahoma.

One of the great Indian orators was a Mingo chief, who was born in 1725 on the banks of the Susquehanna. He refused to take part in Pontiac's war until a band of white men murdered his entire family. On October 10, 1774, Logan joined Shawnee Chief Cornstalk and fought in the Battle of Point Pleasant.

After the battle, the Indians sought peace with Lord Dunmore, governor of Virginia, but Logan was not among them. A messenger was sent to ask Logan to come to the council, but Logan refused and instead sent this reply:

"I appeal to any white man to say if ever he entered Logan's cabin hungry, and he gave him not meat, if ever he came cold and naked, and he clothed him not. During the course of this last long and bloody war, Logan remained in his cabin, an advocate of peace. Such was my love for the whites that my countrymen pointed as they passed by and said, 'Logan is the friend of white man.' I had even thought to have lived with you, but for the injuries of one man, Colonel Cresap, the last spring in cold blood and unprovoked, murdered all the relations of Logan, not even sparing my women and children.

"There was not a drop of blood of any living creature. This called on me for revenge. I have sought, I have killed many, and I have fully glutted my vengeance. For my country, I rejoice at the dreams of peace. But do not harbor a thought that mine is a joy of fear. Logan never felt fear. He will not turn on his heel to save his life. Who is there to mourn for Logan? Not one."

Of his remarkable statement, Thomas Jefferson, in his notes on Virginia said, "I may challenge the whole orations of Demosthenes and Cicero to produce a single passage superior to the speech of Logan, a Mingo chief to Lord Dunmore."

We were impressed by the Gray Wolfs. They brought to the village an added historical dimension. More than that, their costumes were very unusual. Maxine wore bone jewelry, and Gray Wolf dressed more elaborately, with bone breastplates, chokers and horsehair roaches. His style and eloquent voice were admired and appreciated by everyone.

But they didn't finish the season. They were obviously looking for something more. Before coming to our village, Gray Wolf and Chief Running Elk, an Oneida, had started a club on the West Coast. They had opened a trading post called The Longhouse and sold crafts typical of the different tribes who belonged.

Gray Wolf and Running Elk were both well-known for their activities in the League of North American Indians, an organization formed to promote brotherhood and cooperation among all North American tribes.

Their dream was to find some land in West Virginia, eastern Kentucky, southern Pennsylvania or Ohio. They hoped to open a trading post and present programs during the summer and fall months. According to a profile that he left us, there were twelve or fifteen in the group ready to join them. Once they were settled, others would follow. With their energies, intelligence and classic good looks and charm, I hope they realized their dreams. Somehow, I believe they did.

Lightfoot

Sam Lossiah, a Cherokee whose Indian name was Lightfoot, soon joined our colorful parade, wearing a full regalia of eagle feathers and fringed buckskins. Lightfoot was not typical; he was a showman who walked to the tune of jingling bells that hung from his belt, providing his own special drama. He posed for pictures, chased children with a spear and a war-whoop and danced to the hypnotic beat of a rawhide drum. He loved these high-powered performances—and so did the tourists.

But not quite everyone accepted the close proximity of Indian culture. Years later I received a jarring letter from a doctor friend:

Just had to write a note...as I donned my leather moccasins, still comfortable and intact, which I purchased from an Indian Village back in the early 60s from such a unique couple, the owners. The mocs are the same light tan color, still soft, and except for a few spatters of paint, as good as new. Don't recall if I ever told you and Carlo about a unique set of circumstances that took place about then. Sampson Lossiah was an in-patient at the hospital when I admitted another elderly gentleman to the same room and to the only available bed. He was the great-great-great grandson of the original Daniel Boone. Well, just a few hours afterward, I was summoned by the nurses to calm Mr. Boone. He was apparently very upset about having been put in the same room with an INDIAN!!! I tried to calm him, but he was not in any mood to accept his situation. Finally I gruffly informed him that if he didn't quiet down immediately, I'd put him into bed with his new roommate!

Before coming to our village in 1957, Lightfoot had suffered greatly. His young family had perished in a fire caused by a coal oil explosion in their cook stove which burned his house to the ground. Earlier his father had lost both hands in an accident. Being the oldest son, Lightfoot worked hard on the land for his family, and from the stories he shared of home, they all seemed very close. Lightfoot was a thoughtful person. It seemed that his long years of hardship had resulted in softness and a concern for others.

From the time he came to our village until he left several years later, he always looked out for the safety of our little ones. He watched carefully and called out warnings whenever they ventured too near the highway or the river. He taught Dusty to arm wrestle and to perform a war dance. And when Jon was small, he lifted him high above his head and carried him around in the palm of one hand. Our children loved and respected Lightfoot, who had little education, but was gentle and wise. When he was a child, he told us, the teachers tried to assimilate the Indian children into the white man's culture, and if they spoke in their native tongues at school, they got their mouths washed out with soap. That was long ago. Now they were taught to be proud of their heritage and to keep alive the skills of their forefathers.

Lightfoot was not a craftsman, but he had his own talent. He knew everything he needed to know to live in harmony with both people and nature. He could track animals for both food and sport. Once he raised a bear from a small cub that grew to weigh over five hundred pounds. He talked about this bear a lot and said he wished it were here at the village. Thinking it would be a good attraction, we built a large cage and had the bear brought over from the reservation.

Smoky's coat was unbelievably black and shiny. His eyes were small and beady, and he had a giant appetite, especially for soft drinks. He stood on his hind legs and held bottles of coke in his two front paws, a trick the tourists thought was charming.

But one day Smoky got out of his cage and went on a shameless rampage. He chased the workmen up onto the roof of the house, and in a mad frenzy, he broke into the basement of the store and opened up several bags of cement mix, filling the air with clouds of swirling dust that soon covered the ground. Then he walked up and down the busy highway, stopping traffic. After an hour or so of exhilarating freedom, he padded quietly back into his cage, hopped upon his bed and just looked around as if to say, "Hey, look at me!" Lightfoot was quick to point out how smart bears really were.

The season was moving right along, with travelers stopping from both north and south, and as a bonus, we were already seeing plenty of repeat customers. Our business was building even faster than we had anticipated. By now exhausted from the long hours, Carlo had started taking an afternoon nap or a short drive.

One hot afternoon I rode along. We spotted Lightfoot walking down the highway, heading south. Somehow I knew it had something to do with his family. When we stopped him, we learned that his father had fallen gravely ill and that he was going home. Fortunately, our son Buzz was driving by then, so he transported Lightfoot the rest of the way back to the reservation.

We learned later that when he first received the sad news, he entered the store, removed his feathered headdress, and with moccasined feet walked quietly out the door and headed in the direction of Cherokee, a hundred seventy miles away. We knew that if he hadn't found a ride, he would have walked the entire distance.

Lightfoot was a great storyteller with an even greater imagination. It seemed that he saw a strange happening one night, and he came into the store the next morning to inquire whether I had seen it too. Around midnight, he said, he saw big balls of fire up in the mountains. They rolled down toward the highway. Lightfoot waved his arms for emphasis. I reassured him that it was probably foxfire—a fungus that formed on dead wood, giving it a phosphorus glow in the dark. He shook his head in dismay, pushed up his bonnet to cool his forehead and walked back outside to the music of the beating tom-tom.

I enjoyed hearing his stories, but thought that he might have embellished some of the time. Still, who was I to question him? He was of a different culture in an alien environment. So I listened to whatever he had to say, nodded in agreement and thereby made a lifelong friend. Years later when I visited him on the reservation, he told me, "I pray for you whenever I drop to my knees." And to Buzz he once declared, "You are big and strong now. I fought for you when you were little. Now you can fight for me."

Every day Lightfoot posed for pictures and forged new connections. At times we thought he got lonely, so we were delighted when we suspected a romance between him and the pretty, young Cherokee bead maker, Annie, who wore colorful bracelets and daisy chain necklaces.

One morning when we opened the store, Annie came in with a disgruntled look on her face and declared, "Those old white girls won't leave Sam alone." Then she turned and headed back down into the village.

One typical afternoon not long afterward, the tourists were milling around the grounds, taking pictures, drinking Cokes and in general enjoying themselves. This was a very busy season, and we were grateful. Suddenly, a single gunshot was heard. Lightfoot fell to the ground. A bullet had passed just under his bonnet and grazed his scalp, leaving him more frightened than injured. Carlo rushed outside, and when he saw that Lightfoot wasn't hurt, he picked him up and carried him into the store, then laid him down on the floor in front of the moccasin rack. He looked so small, lying there decorated in his arm bustles, breech clout, bells and moccasins.

I was hysterical. The possibility of a tragedy and the ensuing scandal rose up like a black cloud. We closed our doors, but strangely, customers continued to walk around and shop as if nothing startling had occurred. One lady, I remember, even leaned across Lightfoot's body and hunted for a specific shoe style.

The shooting, it turned out, was committed by the teenage son of the white woman he had been seeing.

Soon afterward, Lightfoot left the village, returned home to the reservation and built a small house on his father's property. He then started a new family. Apart from his genius in welcoming and entertaining visitors, there was little change in our atmosphere. We just missed him.

When I visited him last summer, he showed me a twelve-foot embankment that had taken him seven years to dig out by hand. Even at his advanced age and nearly deaf, Lightfoot was still performing hard labor. Then he showed me his beautiful flower garden and declared, "Lucille, when I'm gone, don't send me any flowers." He looked upward toward the sky and waved his arms. "Where I'm going, there will be plenty of flowers for me."

Like Lightfoot, I've come to believe in giving flowers to my friends while they are still living. And whenever an adventure such as a trip presents itself, I go, regardless of any physical infirmities. As my friend Edith Feltner puts it, "You won't hurt any worse there than you will at home."

Just a few weeks ago I visited Lightfoot once more. This time Carcille and Betsy went along. Upon seeing us together, after a warm greeting, Lightfoot hung his head and cried in remembrance of Carlo. Then he got up and walked slowly into the garden and brought back to each of us a long-stemmed red dahlia.

Entrepreneurship Along U.S. 25

*T*he black pickup moved slowly and with quiet dignity into the parking area, then reversed and turned to face the highway. It arrived regularly, loaded with oak split-baskets and ladder-back chairs that hung on each side of the truck bed with such volume that it looked like fresh-baked bread that had risen too much. All of this was presided over by Lillie Elkins, a tiny old lady who wore a long apron and flowered sunbonnet, dipped Bruton snuff and read the Bible between sales.

This entrepreneur from Woodbury, Tennessee, had parked in the very same spot even before we'd purchased the property. She'd made her family's living since the early 1930s by leaving home long before sunrise and traveling up and down the highway, selling her chairs and baskets. She'd raised twelve children and had as many grandchildren, some of whom made these trips with her and her son Richard, who was now doing the driving.

By today's standards she'd had a hard life, rising each day at four a.m., weaving baskets, bottoming chairs and driving long hours to see her many customers. But there she was, spry and happy, still refusing to engage in any business activities on Sundays. She cheered me up with tales of her life and of her big Sunday dinners with family and friends under an old oak tree that stood in her front yard back in Woodbury. There must have been something comforting, I thought, about working within the rhythm of the seasons, knowing that spring, summer and fall were her busy times, and that the winter months were hers to sit at home by the fire.

Once Lily gave me a quilt that she had pieced by hand. I hardly knew how to accept such a lovely gift, so I folded it neatly and put it away in a box. Later she asked me if I were using it. I replied that no, I was saving it for my new house. She tilted her head to one side, smiled, pursed her lips with squinted eyes and said, "Of course, if you don't use it, some other woman will."

The quilt has been worn out now for years.

One afternoon, as I was walking into the store, I caught sight of a brand new black pickup loaded with baskets and chairs pulling into the parking area. It was Lily. Peering at the shiny truck, I inquired about it, knowing that the other one was still in mint condition. Her reply: "I've fixed flats all of my life, and I told myself years ago that if I ever had enough money, I would never fix another. So now, when the tires wear out, I just buy a new truck."

Driving along U.S. 25, we couldn't help noticing new businesses that seemed to spring up overnight. This was the age for traveling. The Great Migration that flourished from 1940 to 1960 unraveled and rewove the fabric of America—with Appalachia losing over one million people to northern cities such as Cincinnati, Cleveland, Chicago, Baltimore and Detroit. All were seeking the economic benefits of urban life.

The roads were smoother, new ones had been built, and families who had gone north to find work in factories or other industries still longed for the mountains and their kinfolk back home. So, with new cars in their driveways, they took to the highways on weekends and holidays. They didn't care about the hairpin mountain curves, the slow-moving town traffic or the lack of automotive air-conditioning. They wanted to go home, and they did so in a steady procession. Heading back north, they filled their trunks with fresh produce their parents had grown in their gardens, and I was often invited to go outside and take a peek. Then I'd be offered a juicy tomato or a just-picked ear of corn.

We soon came to realize that most of our customers were from eastern Kentucky and farther south. They were of our own culture, so it was easy and enjoyable talking to them. Once inside the store, we made certain to greet everyone and to introduce them to others who were standing close by. This created a sense of hospitality, and I've had people tell me that they felt as if they were in my living room. Seldom did anyone leave here a stranger. You sometimes felt you were isolated from the rest of the world, but you weren't. You became a part of people's adventures, their vacation trips, their families—through their selections of jackets and artifacts and souvenirs to take back home and of whatever they were doing at the moment. I quickly discovered that

I had a talent for remembering people's hometowns—and oddly, their shoe sizes—although I couldn't always come up with their names.

Soon we began attracting visitors from as far away as the east and west coasts and even from some foreign countries. How fortunate we were, we thought, to have such rich experiences with so many people without even leaving home. When I stepped outside I was always amazed to see the different license plates and makes and models of cars. One woman actually rode down in her chauffeured Rolls Royce from Dayton, Ohio, to buy deerskin moccasins. Rockcastle River was a halfway point for her to meet her sister and niece in Atlanta.

Travelers who came down our little mountain valley were interested equally in its rugged beauty and romantic history. We were impressed by the different landscapes and the variety of local attractions: Cumberland Gap National Park, where many brave frontiersmen like Daniel Boone, Dr. Thomas Walker, Skaggs and Harrod forged into the unknown wilderness in the late 1700s and opened up Kentucky.
Cumberland Falls State Park, with the thunder of the Cumberland River as it plunged sixty feet within a setting of timeless beauty. On moonlit nights visitors could enjoy walks along wooded trails, down to the falls' precipice to view a "moon bow" created by the full moon's light reflecting against the rising mist. The only other place in the world known to have a moon bow is Victoria Falls, Africa.

Levi Jackson State Park was where the Fort Sequoyah Indian cast presented a reenactment of McNitts Defeat, a bloody massacre by the Shawnee and Chicamauga that killed twenty-four whites on the night of October 3, 1786. Renfro Valley is the second oldest country music show in America, with continuous stage performances. Add The Music Hall of Fame, historic homes, seasonal festivals, Bluegrass horse farms and Berea, the crafts capital of Kentucky.

The caves in our county also held a great fascination for our children, especially the boys, as they were growing up. Over and over, they braved the rocky elements in pursuit of adventure. Although the Great Saltpeter Cave had six miles of channels, it offered no challenge to them. They preferred the more dangerous caves, the Sinks of Roundstone and Climax.

Legend claims that in 1792, John Baker and his wife explored Saltpeter by torchlight. While they were deep inside, their torch went out, and for two days they felt their way from room to room. This was five years before the rich deposits of saltpeter, the chemical from which nitre is extracted and used in the manufacture of gunpowder, were discovered. It was so valuable to hunters that during the War of 1812 sixty men were employed in digging the ore, extracting the nitre and packing homemade shell casings. This ammunition went on muleback to various army camps. After the war, the demand dropped, and only hunters' guns created any market. The Civil War used higher powered explosives, so there was little demand, and the workmen drifted away, closing the first industry in Rockcastle County. We sent visitors from the village there for many years, but now the Cave is open only for special events two or three days annually.

Our single business disadvantage, as we were finding out, was our remote location. Yet we felt it was places like ours, tucked between other larger points of interest, that brought visitors back year after year.

We continually worked hard to create a beautiful store. The inside was rustic, with a potbellied stove (later replaced by a coal furnace), plank floors, wood-paneled walls and open ceiling beams. Hanging from these beams were Navajo rugs, sarapes, baskets, furs such as wolf, fox and beaver, elaborate headdresses and country hams. Tables and shelves were filled with pottery, deerskin jackets (some of which could be made and beaded to order), honey and molasses, shuck beans, dried apples and fresh-ground cornmeal. We had our own gristmill, where Carlo was the miller.

One morning his elderly, hearing-impaired grandfather dropped by and inquired about his grandson's whereabouts. I told him Carlo was out in the mill house, grinding cornmeal. He asked if it were yellow or white. I replied that white corn was all we ever used. He replied, "Yeller is the richest. You can get a quart more to the bushel." He was referring, of course, to moonshine.

We were determined to make a success of our enterprise, to offer unusual things, and we did. It was no accident. Once we hired good management, we could leave the store in capable hands, take our children on trips across the country and visit different Indian reservations for new ideas and to study their culture. We were still eager to travel and learn.

Our showcases were soon lined with silver and turquoise jewelry, expertly crafted and fashioned in exquisite designs. These works of art were made by the Navajo and Zuni Indians. We also bought jewelry from an old trader in Algodones, New Mexico. He shipped it to us in Ball-Mason fruit jar boxes, which I picked up at the Livingston and London train depots. After we'd made our selections, we'd send the rest back. How trusting—and how fortunate for us to have established this kind of relationship early in our business years.

When we first opened the village, Carlo would say that the Indians had finally come back to their Happy Hunting Grounds. In prehistoric times several tribes had roamed Kentucky. Many historians believed they named the area after the wild turkey and river cane that were both so abundant. They called it Kane-Turke. Evidence of campsites and burial grounds are still scattered throughout the landscape, especially under cliffs and near waterfalls. The Indians followed the rivers and valleys, so even today, wherever erosion or plowing occurs, arrowheads and tomahawks are found by amateurs and professionals alike.

My husband had a fine collection himself, although he didn't always have the pleasure of excavating things. Once people learned of his interest, they brought pieces to the store for sale or trade. Carlo displayed them in cases for everyone to enjoy. His collection was later featured in a book, *Who's Who in American Artifacts*.

One day he was in an exceptionally good mood. He had just bought six head sculptures of hard sandstone and of life-size dimensions from a man who claimed to have found them in a cave on the Virginia and Kentucky border. It was a dramatic purchase. Carlo had never seen anything quite like them, and he was excited to add them to his collection.

We put them on display in old oak glass counters, knowing nothing about their origins. One was Sphinx-like with each ear of different configurations. The right ear was closed, and the larger left one had a hole in the middle. The hyena or jackal head looked as if it had been broken off, and "1707" was carved on the bottom. The man said it had been used as a doorstop. Others were human beings wearing feathered headdresses. One appeared to be a chief with the letters "F O" carved on the back. "1711" was carved on the smallest sculpture.

Tourists passed those cases, but they paid no more attention to them than to any other piece we had on display.

Then one day, Vernon and Annette Calhoun from Corbin stopped by. Mr. Calhoun was an educator, and he was intrigued. He had seen a similar sculpture, owned by a man in Tennessee, who told him that it had been plowed up in a field near Norton, Virginia. He grew excited, and with Carlo's permission, his wife Annette drew sketches and then sent them to Dr. Barry Fell, professor at Harvard University and president of the Epigraphic Society.

Dr. Fell responded: "Mr. Calhoun referred the sculptures and inscriptions to me before my Libyan expedition. At that time I was unsure as to the affinity of the work and directed inquiries to Cherokee tribunal authorities through the intermediacy of Colonel Robert Vincent, the Cherokee member of the American Advisory Committee of the Epigraphic Society. It was established that the Cherokee declare the work to be not of their ancestors."

Study of records made by LePage du Pratz (Histoire de la Louisione, 1758) disclosed the following: The Natchez tribe, now extinct, formally extended its boundaries to the Lower Mississippi. The leaders of the Natchez were called "Suns." They wore feathered headdresses similar to the Northern Plains Indians, and the ancestors of the Natchez came to North America from North Africa crossing the Atlantic in the manner that was recorded for the Carthaginians, who employed Libyan mariners and soldiers during the Punic Wars with Rome. Evidence of Carthaginian presence in Libya led Dr. Fell to conclude that the inscriptions on the sculptures represent ancient Natchez Suns, and that they were carved when the Natchez still used Libyan Ogam script. They lived in Kentucky and Virginia, which later became home to the Cherokee and other tribes. The inscriptions on the sculptures are in Libyan Ogam.

Kentucky: Virginia:

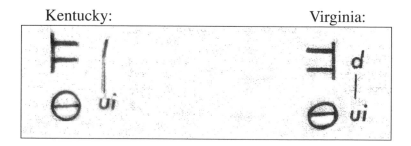

We were continually enthralled by the Native American culture. Theirs was a heritage that could easily have vanished from all historical accounts, due to so much discrimination and maltreatment by our white forefathers. Yet they'd somehow managed through language, customs, crafts and storytelling to preserve it. We were discovering through our business that many Americans genuinely admired both their resilience and their artistry.

By now signs were everywhere along U.S. 25, and Fort Sequoyah had its share. They were nailed to fence posts, old barns and trees: "Country hams, elk and buffalo moccasins, deerskin jackets and gloves." And, "We accept Canadian money." Some of our signs were cut in eye-catching Thunderbird shapes. It was reported that one was seen leaning on a fence corner in southern Indiana.

This decorative stretch of highway extended fifty miles or more, and it looked like a colorful display of yard art. There were gazing balls, chalk dogs, pink flamingos, sets of dishes, baskets, chairs, porch swings, pottery, primitive willow lawn furniture, bright chenille bedspreads and robes that hung on clotheslines. All reflected the expressions of the individual shopkeepers, and all have now faded from the view of the American traveler.

Not surprisingly, our business eventually grew to accommodate an eating establishment—another way, we thought, to attract new customers. We converted the former Deerfoot museum into a Bar-B-Q ranch with lots of windows. Saddle stools from Texas lined a polished knotty pine counter with bridles hanging from cedar posts along the countertops. The large brick oven had mirror-like steel doors and could hold up to two or three hams and several chickens. It was built on the principle of an old-fashioned step stove with hickory wood smoke curling around and through the meat. For those who love Bar-B-Q, there is nothing that tastes (or smells) better.

The wide brick chimney was an attraction in itself, with antique cast iron pots and kettles sitting on top of the pit. Saddles hung on the walls, and horse collars inside the windows held lighted lanterns. Picnic tables and benches were lacquered to a high gloss against wood floors. The name Fort Sequoyah was cattle-branded in fancy script on the tabletops.

Our Bar-B-Q ribs, pork, beef and chicken were all served with French fries, hush puppies and cole slaw. We also offered fish sandwiches and country ham—and for dessert, fresh-baked apple pie. Plain and simple. Young, pretty servers wore cowboy hats and boots.

The western touch, right in the middle of nowhere, distinguished it from other area restaurants. But Bar-B-Q did not catch on too well with the locals. We were lucky to have the tourist traffic. And Dusty, our four-year-old, discovered the pathway behind our store to the restaurant and suddenly developed a great love for fish sandwiches. He went every single day for weeks and ordered two fish sandwiches "to go." Was he really eating them? We decided to find out. One day his grandfather, the proprietor, followed him. He found Dusty sitting on a big rock, eating one sandwich and feeding the other to his dog, B.J.

We wondered if perhaps that was the only sandwich that he knew how to order.

The landscape around the buildings was blacktop, dotted with covered wagons, teepees and hitching posts. And trees, always plenty of trees, and in the springtime, colorful wildflowers growing along the riverbank.

People seemed to enjoy coming here, and that, of course, was the reward for our hard work.

When you are in your twenties, trying to raise a family and build a business at the same time, all co-mingling, you sometimes stop and ask yourself, "Why did I come here?" But who would not come to the magic and charm of this place to hear the whippoorwill call, the owls hoot, and the singing tree frogs at nightfall? Every day was a new experience at the village, and some were unforgettable.

Three young boys came into the store, looked around and then made some purchases. They paid me with a handful of silver coins. An hour later they returned and bought more. Again, they paid in silver. The old money attracted my attention. Nobody after 1964 would be paying with that kind of cash; something was obviously wrong. I stared as they left and felt a moment of panic when I did not see them get into a car. Instead they crossed the highway and walked into the woods. I called the police.

Soon my phone began ringing. My suspicions proved correct. Three boys who looked to be no older than twelve to fourteen years of age were missing, along with a car and a cache of old coins. I later learned that they had stolen their neighbor's car and driven some distance north on I-75 before running off the road and driving into a ditch. They just abandoned the car and walked to exit 49, then came on down to our village. I do not remember who showed up first, the parents or the police officers, but I do remember returning the coins for an even exchange in money.

The bus on the beach in Florida. Carcille (holding Jon), Buzz and Dusty.

Highway scene at Bar-B-Que Ranch at Fort Sequoyah.

My children with playmates.

Betsy and Koula with their Christmas hats and muffs.

A Cherokee Indian

Flaming Arrow (James Paytiamo), silversmith from Acoma, New Mexico.

LaRue Paytiamo, 91 years young.

*Lillie Todd Elkins and grandson,
Bill Elkins (part-time driver).*

Dusty in street scene at Riverboat Town.

John in front of old shop.

FORT SEQUOYAH
INDIAN VILLAGE

U. S. 25, Midway London, Ky. - Mt. Vernon, Ky·

Fort Sequoyah Indian Village is located on Dixie Highway, U S. 25 in the heart of Scenic Cumberlands Wonderland, where Daniel Boone blazed his first trail among the Indians into Kentucky in 1775 Later retracing his trail to found Boonesboro, Ky.

Less than 35 miles from Berea, Ky., home of the famous Paul Green drama, "Wilderness Road", June 30 - Sept. 1 at the Indian Fort Theatre

Points of interest near by: Levi Jackson State Park, Wildernss Road State Park, Pioneer Memorial State Park, Cumberland Falls, Lake Cumberland and Cumberland Gap National Park.

Only 15 miles from Historic Renfro Valley Settlement, home of well-known radio broadcasts over MBS and CBS radio networks.

Out of the aboriginal past comes the re-creation of this Cherokee Indian village of 1750 so posterity can see what life was like before the white man blazed these happy hunting grounds.

HERE in the Fort, Cherokee Indian men and women daily carry on an ancient way of life, practicing the centuries-old arts of basket-weaving, cooking, pottery, weapon-making and bead-

Old poster – 1955.

Right: Scene at Fort Sequoyah showing use of blowgun.

Below: Indian dance at Fort Sequoyah.

Chief Lightfoot

Cast members at Fort Sequoyah.

Chief Lone Fox

Basket splits in beginning stage.

Seven Sided Council House, Fort Sequoyah, scene 1955 or 1956.

Potter at village.

Council House in village.

Carlo and Lucille Carloftis, Fort Sequoyah.

The Blacksmith Shop today.

Another day, an elegant relative Mary Muncy dropped by. Together we walked down to the house. When she was ready to leave, she paused at the front door, and I was chagrined to notice for the first time in a long while that there was no grass whatsoever around my patio. The ground was worn as smooth and as flat as a pancake. I had seen her beautiful home and flower gardens, so viewing the place through her eyes, I apologized: "We've never been able to grow any grass here." Her gaze swept across all of the little cars and toy trucks lying around. She took my hands in hers and gently replied, "But you are growing boys now."

One afternoon a woman strolled into the store and said she just wanted to stretch her legs and browse. She walked around in slow motion, looking with polite interest at different styles of moccasins, and then she moved on to the next display. Time went by, and her husband appeared in the doorway. He beckoned that he was ready to leave. But she insisted on staying a little longer, saying she would catch him in a minute. She kept looking, and he kept waiting. Finally with great deliberation, he shouted, "If you don't come right now, you'll be catching a Greyhound bus!"

On another afternoon a chartered bus pulled in and parked at the end of the drive. It was the Glenn Miller Band! I had danced to their tunes as a teenager, and now, here they were, showing up to enjoy our Bar-B-Q beef. I did my best to stay calm. Another time, Tennessee Ernie Ford stopped by with his family. After browsing the store, they all purchased pairs of moccasins. When he approached the counter to pay, he introduced us to his wife and two sons. I was excited and thought he was far more handsome, standing there in his casual yellow T-shirt, than he'd ever appeared on TV.

But I was not the only one who caught celebrity fever. An elderly man approached him and declared nervously, "I know who you are! You're Henry Ford." Tennessee Ernie wrapped one arm around the fellow's shoulder and replied, "Old partner, I wish I were."

Playtime

O ur children were fast becoming free spirits. They played hard—climbing trees, swinging on vines, wading the branch and strolling the grounds like tiny tourists, wearing sunglasses and stringing toy cameras and binoculars around their necks. They darted from one adventure to another, stopping only long enough to eat and sleep.

They made mud pies in Coke bottle caps, constructed purses and billfolds from the cardboard collars that came from laundered shirts and built playhouses from the large boxes in which our merchandise arrived.

The girls formed rag hair curlers from strips of brown bags. They went to bed, still wearing those paper twigs, and when they fell asleep and moved their heads on the pillows, the sound effects were like a rattling fire.

Our three daughters shared one room, but each had her own Jenny Lind cherry twin bed. The overhead rafters were left exposed, and it was from these that they practiced their exercise skills, imagining themselves trapeze artists, flying around the room and landing in safety nets—their soft beds.

Once Koula and Betsy overloaded the washer with dishwashing liquid, and then let the suds bubble and overflow. I came into the house, heard the giggles and discovered them "skating" on the wet, slippery floor.

Our children had time, energy, patience and freedom. If it rained they played inside or rehearsed a skit to perform for us at the end of our long workday. Sometimes they'd rearrange our furniture. One day they piled the sofa cushions onto the floor and then noticed a tag which read, "Do Not Remove." They found the scissors and cut it off, then got scared and wandered morosely into the store to admit what they had done.

More often, I discovered their latest mischief only when Koula would slip a folded note into Carlo's hand, relating who had just spilled or broken what—or else she'd get Betsy to deliver it for her. We hired help for daily housekeeping chores and asked them to keep an eye on the children, but all six of them clearly preferred to be left alone.

We had surely found the perfect location. No other home or business faced the immense beauty of the mountains, the river and the natural, wooded landscape. Also, since we were connected to the national forest and on U.S. 25, we were guaranteed many passing travelers. But we were seeing more every day the added benefits of living where our little ones could play outside.

"Where are the children?" Mama would ask me whenever she came to visit. "Are they out on the commons?" That was what she called our property. As shameful as it sounds today, most of the time I had no idea where they were. For the most part, they led an unmonitored, Huckleberry-Finn existence.

But Carlo could whistle. Every so often he'd step out back and make that shrill sound between his teeth—a signal that all of the children needed to show themselves before resuming their play. One day, after giving the signal, he saw two little figures, Carcille and Koula, come marching up from under the riverbank. Then he spotted Buzz, age seven, dragging Betsy, age three, who was literally covered in mud. Buzz had caught her just moments before she might have tumbled into deep water.

Carcille got to play hero one day too. She was four, and Buzz was two. They'd been jumping on one of the beds—when suddenly, he toppled right out of a second-story window. Luckily, Carcille caught him and held onto one of his legs, screaming and crying, as Buzz hung spread-eagled against the house. Carlo raced up the steps and yanked Buzz back inside the bedroom.

Somehow we always seemed to be misplacing Dusty. He had a disconcerting habit of just wandering off. Once, when he was about three, no one could find him. Out of our heads with worry, we finally enlisted our customers' help. Everyone called and called. Nothing. All of the boys had been cautioned about going too near the river, but I knew they did, because they were always bringing me wildflower bouquets.

Finally, in a state of near-panic, I walked back into the store, where we'd stacked a huge pile of cotton bedspreads—and I spotted a tiny boot dangling from a top edge. Dusty had climbed up there and had fallen fast asleep.

As much as they enjoyed exploring, Carcille, Buzz and Koula still talked about their sandbox on Commanche Island. Not wanting to deny them such a simple pleasure, we had a truck dump a load of sawdust over the bank. The three played in it for hours, stuffing sawdust into their socks and shoes, falling down in it, breathless with laughter.

Until the cats found it.

We justified our self-indulgent business focus by letting the children have a virtual barnyard of animals. It all started when Gertrude Mounts, an elegant lady from Livingston, paid us a visit, carrying a box under her arm. It contained a little bantam hen sitting on a nest of twelve tiny eggs.

She made quite a ceremony of her presentation. The children stood and looked at one another, rolling their eyes. Eggs? So what? After several daily inspections, however, the baby chicks finally peeped out of their shells. From there our flock grew to over one hundred hens and crowing roosters. Chickens were never our specialty—but we did enjoy watching the children feed and try to catch them.

The fascination was contagious. Early one morning, three men and a small boy stood in the store's doorway. It was obvious that these were not typical shorts-and-sandals tourists; the men were dressed in coats and ties. As their eyes traveled around the room, one commanded the boy, "Pick out anything you want, and I'll buy it for you." Delighted, I put on my best smile and greeted them warmly.

Slowly we walked around the store. We passed the moccasin rack, and I fitted the child with a pair. Next I showed him spears, tomahawks, feather headdresses, coonskin caps and every other conceivable thing that I thought a young boy might like. I rubbed my eyes in disbelief when nothing seemed to interest him. He dropped a small, sad face. I could tell that his companions were growing weary, and so was I.

They were just about to leave, when suddenly the boy exclaimed, "Here—that's what I want!" He pointed toward the doll table.

"Surely you don't want a doll," the man said.

The boy shook his head no, then pointed down underneath the table and declared, "See? I want that."

It was a little brown chicken that had wandered onto the porch and into the store.

Far from being excited, my reaction was embarrassment. I recovered quickly enough to say that if he could have it, I would catch it for him. It was easy—and together we hunted for a box, cut holes for it to breathe, and then we tied it for its journey home. The boy left, carrying the box and wearing a big smile.

It was not uncommon to see stray dogs and cats wandering the property looking for a home, particularly in the spring and early summer. Often people just dropped them off and then drove away. And since our children loved animals, our collection kept growing. It included mongrel dogs, peacocks, turkeys, roosters, geese, ducks, guineas, rabbits and goats—and a talking, yellow-headed parrot, which had belonged to their grandmother Carloftis in Pineville. The children were all fascinated with a bird that could speak. When it was time for the school bus to arrive in the mornings, it would scream, "Hurry up, Hurry up!" and they would all dart out the door, giggling. Buzz was the only one who could go near its cage without it squawking and grabbing at the first little hand that came within range. One day Jon ignored the warning to stay away and was rushed to the doctor's office with a finger that was nearly bitten off. The scar is still there. Dr. Lewis said that he had never treated that kind of physical injury from a bird bite before.

The children also had a pony, fat and sleek, with deep white spots on its rich, dark brown coat and a flowing honey-colored mane. A fine leather bridle and saddle gave it a handsome, sporty look. Dusty and Jon were so proud. They were especially excited to show it off to their visiting grandmother. So we all lined up, and I led the pony through the front hall and then into the living room where my mother was sitting. At the sight of a horse in the house, Mama gasped and surely thought, "What a silly daughter I have raised!"

We always knew that spring had officially arrived when Jon got out the old wheelbarrow to take his dog Teddy for a ride. Teddy was a sort of Eskimo Spitz with a thick, white coat, whom Jon had raised from a small puppy. It was obvious that he had no pedigree, but that didn't matter to Jon. Teddy was his companion—his pal.

Later on, I kept turkeys, guineas and peacocks in the bed of an old 1954 model international truck that we had used for many years. When they grew old enough, we turned them loose to run wild. One little boy, who loved to come here to watch the birds, called our business The Peacock House.

Buzz delighted in the peacocks too. He threw corn up on the roof of our sun porch and fed them, watching them strut their glorious colors––until one day our roof began leaking like a sieve. Suddenly, that all stopped.

One tom turkey became oddly possessive of me. If I walked outside the store and over to the house, he'd appear out of nowhere from behind the pots and plants, drumming and strutting. Sometimes he took the shortcut through the woods and would be there by the time I was.

You cannot reason with an aggressive turkey. One day, flogging and spurring, he chased a man up the front steps of our store. An attorney friend told me that if I didn't get rid of that turkey, someone else would soon own our business. So Tom was sent away, and from all reports, he was a very happy bird once he got to the farmyard.

A little later, as the season wore on, we bought a train that would carry thirty children at one time. It had been running in one of the parks in Louisville, and we were intrigued by its loud whistle and clanging bell. While the train was being loaded for its journey home, Mrs. Hammer, the owner's wife, decided to teach me to knit. She gave me needles and a skein of turquoise wool to work on as we drove from Louisville. I would love it, she said. I'll make my children scarves, I thought. But by the time I got home, I had lost the stitch and settled for a little cream pitcher that she had given me. I still have it.

Never had the village been filled with more enthusiasm than when everyone saw that train. It attracted the attention of local children as well as the tourists. We hired Albert Mounts, a retired railroader, and Junior Jones to act as conductor and engineer. Albert wore a blue-and-white striped cap and red kerchief and waved to the little children who were standing in line to catch the next ride.

So many of our passions, it seems now, were brief excursions. When the girls were old enough to wear pantyhose, Carlo, who liked to bargain, was delighted when a salesman dropped by with an assortment of colored hosiery. "The newest trend," he said. Cheaper by the dozen? No, cheaper by the gross! Surprises fell out of boxes, as the girls were introduced to the concept of "seconds," with legs either too long or too short, often on the very same pair. But such minor flaws did not squelch their excitement; they went through them like candy at Christmas—opening a new pair nearly every day, choosing from exciting hot colors--pink, blue, green, yellow and orange. Did they last long enough to be laundered? Of course not. New became old in the course of a single day as each pair was tossed into the waste can. Cheaper by the gross? No, as it turned out, not this time.

Despite the abnormal lack of rules and restrictions, our children were generally considerate of others and very conscientious. Dusty and Jon loved to play cards in the morning while they waited for the school bus. One day, after Dusty had left the room, Jon got up from the table and came over to the sink, where I was washing the breakfast dishes. "Momma, I'm sick," he declared, pressing his little head against my leg.

"What's wrong, Honey?" I asked.

He came right out with it. "When Dusty went to the bathroom, I peeked at his cards."

"Well," I responded, "that's easy to fix. Just tear up the board, tell him what happened, and start over."

Which they did. Soon the school bus arrived, and they both ran to catch it, laughing as they went.

By now we had added two more rooms to our house to accommodate our ever-growing family. Each one was large with still more windows. No partitions for us. We wanted to bring the beauty of the outdoors into our home, so it was a garden house with full outside views.

One evening, after a particularly busy day, Carlo and I looked at each other and decided it was time to close. It was getting dark outside, and the cars had all gone from the parking area. We locked up, headed toward the house, then stopped and stood for a moment in the shadows of the security lights and looked down toward it.

Lone Fox appeared out of nowhere. "Just like the Oklahoma Indians," he remarked softly. "They turn on all the lights in their homes, then go out to stand on the hillside—and look in."

Our Lives Are Touched

*L*one Fox was a full-blooded Yuma Indian from Arizona—which he always claimed was the hottest place on Earth. His long, salt-and-pepper hair was parted in the middle and pulled back behind his ears. He wore a Western shirt set off by a turquoise bolo and a large turquoise belt buckle with wide silver cuff bracelets on both arms. He strutted and swaggered around in his loose-fitting slacks and black cowboy boots—a throwback, we suspected, from the romantic days when he followed the Wild West shows.

I asked what he was doing here. He said he was a friend of one of the bead makers whom he had met on the reservation in North Carolina. No one ever knew exactly how long he would stay, but one thing was sure. Everyone was pleased to see Lone Fox drive up in his van.

He was a talented showman who knew how to draw a crowd. He held us captive with stories of famous Indians he had worked with. There was a pleasant and comfortable rhythm in his voice.

Lone Fox was also an old-style medicine man. In addition to his pitch on the curative powers of herbal healing, he could cut a cigarette out of a man's mouth in a flash with his bull whip. He performed other magical tricks to a cheering audience. Passing cars would screech their wheels to a stop before pulling off the road.

Buzz, then an elementary school student, began taking flute lessons. He remembers Lone Fox showing a keen interest in his flute-playing, saying that he had played the clarinet in the U.S. Navy band many decades earlier. Betsy, not much older than a toddler, was also glad to see him come. Lone Fox would lift her up on the store's counter, admire her thick, glossy, black hair, and say, "Sing, Betsy, sing." Then they would sing together, her bright, high voice piping, "My country, tis of thee…"

Long after the village had closed, and the Indians had gone back to the reservation, we received a visit from Lone Fox. He wanted to give me a skirt, he said. It was a long, gold-colored brushed woolen with intricate decorative designs along the hem. Obviously, a treasured museum piece. He left shortly thereafter, saying he was on his way to King's Mountain, Tennessee, and this would be his last trip north. We hated to see him go, and for days afterward, I kept wishing that I had asked him about the skirt's origin. It was definitely a one-of-a-kind.

We never heard from Lone Fox again, but to this day I have the skirt.

All of us were learning what it was like to have people moving in and out of our lives. Some became fast friends. Others were only briefly enjoyable as days, weeks, months and years sped by. My life was romanced by not only different cultural styles, but by people's stories too.

A couple entered the store. As always I greeted them warmly and made polite talk. I showed them around and presented a brief history of our business.

The husband worked at the Department of Fish and Wildlife in Frankfort. I told them of the time that Dusty, then eight, came rushing in and announced that he wanted to be a game warden when he grew up. When I asked why, he replied, "Because Freddie Noe and Mr. Elkins (the game wardens) are always laughing whenever I see them."

The wife then told me what their son, about the same age, had said to them. They had taken him to one of the Capitol buildings in Frankfort. He looked around and was impressed, appreciative and beaming. Then he declared, "When I grow up I want to be a janitor!"

We recall stories about animals we have known as well.

Boy was a little brown dog—a mongrel, a breedless breed. Yet he had a better brain than many of his more aristocratic relatives. He was shrewd, active and strong, well-equipped for any struggle.

He also had a strange wild streak, and he showed no desire to be friends with us. He ate the food we set out, but declined to enter the puppy house that sat empty at the far side of our home. All attempts to pet him were failures. He shunned us, darting from one spot to another, peeping around the corners of buildings, or else he sat crouched, half hidden beneath the creeping hemlock branches.

It was obvious that Boy had been mistreated. We wondered where he had come from and how he had managed to escape more punishment. After much pain on our behalf and more on his, he began to tolerate us. But he would never come close enough for us to touch him.

After a full year, by chance we might pat his head or with a free hand, stroke his chest. If we touched his back, however, he ran away. At other times he wagged his tail and leaped high into the air.

He was constantly on the prowl, checking the property. We'd hear his nervous bark whenever he encountered something unusual or when he dashed across the pasture in hot pursuit of the miniature horses, Uncle and Nephew. He was once caught posing on the foot bridge along with Jon's two pampered pups, Daisy and Bertha, thereby making the cover of Jon's book, *First a Garden.*

But early that summer we noticed the collar he was wearing seemed too tight. Should we try to catch him to remove it? Put something in his food to make him drowsy? We tried both. Nothing worked.

During that same summer while Buzz was mowing the lawn, Boy trotted up to him and thrust his neck forward. Buzz reached down and quickly unbuckled his collar. Boy turned and ran away.

One morning before opening the store, I arrived home from the post office in Livingston to discover that a pack of stray dogs had wandered in off the highway. I opened the car door just in time to see them tearing savagely at Boy. In vain he fought to hold them off, but they had him nailed between the cars and the carriage house walls. He couldn't escape. Gasping and writhing, he fell to the ground. As soon as he regained his wits, he crawled to seek cover under the wisteria plants.

With tears falling, Betsy and I patted his head and looked into his soft brown eyes. Buzz gently wrapped him in a woolen blanket for his ride to the veterinarian.

Poor Boy. He was a true hero, who without a thought touched our lives. He lived and did his very best in his own little world...and then died.

LaRue

W̲e̲ were coming into contact with so many different cultures. People seemed literally to weave in and out of our lives. Over the years that tapestry extended even further, into second and third generations. The word had spread. As a "destination" with a far-reaching reputation, we welcomed everyone into our store as graciously as we would into our home.

The Paytiamos arrived one perfect spring morning in 1957, driving a late-1930s black Chevrolet coupe filled with all of their belongings. Flaming Arrow was a full-blooded Pueblo Indian from Acoma, New Mexico, and his wife LaRue was white. As they strode aggressively down the walk toward our house, I noticed that she was much older than her husband—as it turned out, eighty to his sixty. Short and plump, with silvery curls peeking around a close-fitting hat with colorful appliqués of pink, purple and yellow, she had a slight tremor in her hands—noticeable only because of the exquisite turquoise rings and bracelets she wore. It was obvious that she had never been beautiful, not even in her youth, but she had an impressive carriage, and we were instantly captivated by her charm.

Her handsome husband sat beside her on our sun porch sofa, smiling and nodding as she did most of the talking. Bright rays of sunshine streamed through the leafy trees and bounced on the green tiled floors. He gazed at his wife in complete adoration.

Mrs. Paytiamo gave us a brief account of their travels since having come back east, pausing only long enough to enjoy a cup of coffee and, a couple of hours later, a Coke. Our conversation lasted until late morning, and we were delighted when they both seemed to show an extraordinary interest in the Indians already at our village.

LaRue painted local-color oils. She had studied at the Art Institute in

Chicago and with famed animal artist Ernest Thompson Seton in Santa Fe. For four years she had painted prize cattle and horses. There were seventeen of her paintings from Indian sketches of dancers displayed in the Pueblo exhibit at Columbia University. She had also illustrated *Flaming Arrow's People*, written by Flaming Arrow, Indian author and baritone.

Flaming Arrow was a silversmith. He had worked in a Santa Fe hotel, making jewelry for tourists. One of his clients was Mrs. Dodge of the renowned automobile company.

Upon learning that his real name was James, we inquired about the significance of his Indian name. James' grandfather had told him the legend of one of the Kachina gods: A baby boy was born very poor, having no father to support him. The sun shone its rays through the window of the house, giving warmth to the child and his mother. But henceforth, the sun came out only one time each year. As the boy grew, he noticed that other boys lived with their fathers, and he wondered where his had gone. Once he was old enough to travel, he began roaming around, asking everyone. One day his journey took him to the Arrow Maker. "Can you tell me where my father is?" he asked. The Arrow Maker nodded. "I will shoot you into your father's village," he told the boy, "and where the arrow hits the ground, the people will come running and look all around it. You must not come out until they all go back into their homes, or your magic will disappear into them. Only then can you leave the arrow and hunt for a rainbow ladder, which will take you to the house where your father lives."

So the Arrow Maker put the boy inside the arrow, placed the arrow in the bowstring and then fired it. The air's friction made the arrow blaze. The place where it landed was called Sunrise Village. But the arrow was so hot that it took four days before the flame died down, and the boy could leave it. The people watched and named it Flaming Arrow. Even the Medicine Man came to worship this strange object. Oddly, that was the end of the story.

The Native American world view was a continual source of fascination. One late afternoon I walked down to the house past the newly excavated basement of our shop. On the ground I spotted a headdress and a blouse, and beside them Flaming Arrow was lying on the fresh dug dirt with his arms and legs outstretched, facing the sky. When I gasped aloud, he spoke softly: "I'm all right. I'm just soaking up the minerals from the ground into my body."

But it was the Paytiamos' partnership of the heart, despite their age difference, which really intrigued me. They did so many unexpected things together. They even owned a Geiger counter and went on regular expeditions, checking for deposits of uranium and thorium. LaRue told me they had a little box of melted sand from the first atomic bomb site––very rare. I stopped by their cabin one morning, and upon opening the door, a comforting aroma filled my nostrils. It smelled like fresh baked bread just out of the oven. But to my surprise it turned out to be scorched cornmeal still sitting in a pan on the top of the stove. The Paytiamos were going on a short treasure hunt. LaRue would bag up this meal and take it along in case they stayed longer than planned.

After only a week or two at the village LaRue strolled into the store and wanted to know where the nearest library was. She'd quickly discovered that the other women were more interested in Harlequin romances and mail-order catalogs than in good reading material. In the short time that we had known each other, we'd become close friends. I was young, and Mrs. Paytiamo was experienced, educated, free-spirited, well-traveled and well-established. She was a wonderful companion, full of marvelous stories, and we shared hours of memories as we watched the tourists file in and out of the store or enjoyed the pleasure of driving around on hot summer days.

As for her work, Mrs. Paytiamo sat on the porch near the front door, surrounded by the strong odor of the tools of her trade. She painted from memory scenic oils of her beloved West—maybe a cowboy on a horse, a black bear, birds or colorful flowers. She was quite contented to be dabbing at these "bread-and-butter" panels, as she called them. We talked every day, and each encounter was to me like reading a new chapter in an absorbing book. I anxiously awaited every fresh installment.

LaRue was born into and lived the life of an upper middle-class woman until her first husband's death. Her pioneer grandfather Abram Weaver and two other men were the only whites living in the Iowa territory when it was a vast prairie populated by several roaming Indian tribes. They built a few log cabins and named their settlement Bloomfield.

Her grandfather loved and collected rocks, but he could not identify them. There were no libraries with books to help him. LaRue's love of rocks began when she walked through the woods with other children. They came home carrying flowers. She came home carrying rocks. Her father would see her and remark, "Here comes Grandfather Weaver with his rocks."

Her fascination with Indians also began early. One day an Indian who had attended the same university as her father came to visit and stayed a week. Later, when she visited her grandfather in Kansas, he showed her an immense bow as tall as any man. Chief Shagonaby had given it to him as a remembrance of the days they had hunted deer and bison in the forests together.

Meanwhile, her father, Dillon H. Payne, gained a nationwide reputation as a lawyer. He worked on the celebrated case of copper king Andrew J. Davis. The trial attracted great attention because of the millions involved and the celebrity of the attorneys. When the case was finally resolved, he received an unsolicited testimonial which he prized highly.

My Dear Sir:

For several months I have been associated with Dillon H. Payne, Esq. in what is known as the Davis Will case. It gives me great pleasure to state that Mr. Payne has shown himself to be an excellent lawyer with a wide accurate knowledge of the textbooks and the decisions.

He has prepared briefs on many important points, and has prepared them with discrimination and skill. He has also prepared a great portion of the case for trial, and in this work he has shown great skill, industry and sense. I have never associated with any lawyer who did his work in a better and clearer manner. He has always shown himself to be a lawyer of great learning, of great industry and accuracy. I could not recommend him too highly. Besides he is in every way a real gentleman.
I have the honor to remain,
Yours sincerely,
R. H. Ingersall

In 1922 Payne and his wife were appointed by Iowa's governor to travel to Rio De Janeiro for the World's Centennial Exposition. Six people were invited from each state. They sailed from New York City and were gone for nearly three months.

LaRue was trained early to meet the demands of the refined society in which she lived. Although her family was strict, everyone understood and appreciated her love of the outdoors. Nevertheless, she was given piano lessons, and she practiced long and hard every day. If she missed a note, the instructor hit her across the fingers with a stick, making her repeat the exercise until she had mastered it.

Whenever she was mischievous, her mother would lock her in the smokehouse. She would lie down, kick and scream through the crack at the bottom of the door until she knew her mother had gone inside. Then she leaned back and happily entertained herself with the stacks of *Harper's Bazaar* magazines that sat nearby. She said she didn't mind the punishment; she actually enjoyed it—until one day, when she reached over to pick up a magazine, and there sat the biggest spider she had ever seen. Spiders terrified her. She cried for help, but nobody came. From that day on she was careful never to be put in the smokehouse again.

LaRue received a formal education, and in 1898 graduated from Wesleyan College in Mount Pleasant, Iowa, with a degree in music. Her subsequent teaching career was devoted to both music and art. She was also an outstanding pianist, in demand for her musical talents wherever she went.

Eventually she married the banker's son, but they had only a few short years together before he died of epilepsy. Their daughter was given a name that LaRue had always loved as a young girl: Florence. If she'd had a son, she told me wistfully, his name would have been Dustan. Eventually she got her wish. Our little boy became Dustan—Robert Dustan, called Dusty.

After her first husband's death LaRue decided to mark her freedom and independence by leaving the sheltered life she had always known and move from Iowa. Her only sister had married a Methodist minister and settled on the California coast. Unlike her sister, who preferred the finer things, LaRue viewed herself as an explorer, even willing to expose herself to danger if needed.

So she sent resumes across the country in search of a teaching position. The first one she heard from that sounded interesting, she decided, she would take Florence and go. Her first assignment, I believe, was in Paducah, Kentucky. From there she traveled to other parts of the continent, including Canada. She once joked that she was probably the world's earliest hippie.

One day she paused mid-story, her eyes flicking over a couple who had just passed us and demanded, "Why do handsome men marry such ugly women?" At age eighty-plus, she was still fueled by her passionate love for Flaming Arrow, who walked with collected elegance in his snow-white trousers and crimson blouse held at the waist by a woven, braided sash of beige, brown and sky blue. On each arm he wore a large cuff bracelet of silver and turquoise, and his moccasins were buckskin fastened to the side with conch-buckles. He was truly a picture of refined Indian good looks—even at sixty years old. "Isn't he handsome?" she would sigh. "When I first met James, my love bloomed forth."

In 1910 she accepted a position as a music teacher in the Indian schools in Albuquerque, New Mexico—a place teeming with cowboys, ranchers, coyotes, mountain lions and cattle. As a widow she was free to go west and take up a new life where Indians lived. A train carried her across the prairie. She saw her first mountains, so blue in the distance––and there, in the New Mexico railroad station, her first gathering of Indians.

One day that fall, the local auto mechanic's brother from California came to visit. His name was James Paytiamo. He was a full-blooded Pueblo, educated and very good-looking. The mechanic was courting one of the school nurses. LaRue had a car, so all four went for a ride. They drove down to the little village of Isleta, about fifteen miles to the south.

The moon shone like day over the Sandia Mountains to the east. LaRue liked this newcomer. Much later, he revealed to her that a fortuneteller had predicted that his destiny was to marry a schoolteacher––and evidently, here she was.

The next day, she told her nurse friend, "Well, I have found my Indian, but he will go back west, and I will never see him again." Her friend replied, "If he is the right one, then you will." Instead of leaving, James found a job in the city. He came to see LaRue every evening. Three months later they were married. "I became the white wife of a red man," she said, "and for me a most adventurous life began."

LaRue's and my friendship soon developed into a social dimension. Our Eastern Star chapter was hosting a district meeting, and I was in a flurry all afternoon getting ready for it. Since this was the biggest social event in Livingston, everyone who belonged to the order, especially the officers, wore long evening dresses in traditional colors. I asked Mrs. Paytiamo if she knew about the Eastern Star, and her reply was, "I've been a member since 1898." I invited her to go along.

We found a parking space up the street and climbed the stairs to the second-floor lodge hall. Inside we found the hall filled with elegantly dressed men and women moving gracefully, meeting and talking with delegates from other chapters. I knew a lot of them, and I introduced Mrs. Paytiamo. She flipped the scarf that wrapped her shoulders, smiled and declared, "I'm not much to look at—so what do you want to talk about?" From there, she delighted everyone with her witty remarks until the doors closed, and the meeting started.

Surrey trail down to river.

The Paytiamos

The Paytiamos were going south for the winter. They had loaned us a large, beautiful painting of Brice Canyon that LaRue had done years earlier and a white fur rug that I had tacked upon our wooden counter. They came to pick them up and to bid us farewell.

They traveled to south Florida, where we eventually paid Flaming Arrow a short visit in the town where he was employed. We did not see his wife this time. Instead of returning to Kentucky, in 1965 they headed west to Datil, New Mexico. Shortly afterward, Flaming Arrow abruptly died of a heart attack. LaRue blamed the sudden high altitude.

Knowing she would be devastated and all alone, Carlo and I packed up our children and made the drive across the country to try to be of some comfort to her. For five days we took her on a memory trip—and for five days we saw remote, out-of-the-way places which tourists seldom visited.

We went to Acoma, where she and Flaming Arrow had once lived so happily together. LaRue wanted to show us a different civilization than we could ever imagine—as good as going to Europe, she said. She was right. We climbed 367 feet to the top of a mesa called Sky City. At first it looked impossible for her and for us, but by regularly stopping and resting, we slowly made it. Looking over the flat-topped mesa hundreds of feet above the desert floor, I wondered how many times they had stood at that edge and looked at the same sparse growth of rabbit brush, cactus, and juniper. And over into the distance, at the Enchanted Mesa, where no one has ever lived because of its impossibly steep walls.

It was amazing to find ourselves standing on this great, ancient, wind-swept rock that had once held hundreds of families. Most had since migrated downward to Acomita and other nearby villages. Still, there were families living a primitive life, just as their forefathers had before Columbus came to this continent.

The pueblo of Acoma is the oldest continuously inhabited city in the United States. Recently archaeologists theorized that Acoma has been occupied since 1150 AD. In 1540 Francisco Vasquez de Coronado's army visited Acoma and became the first white men ever to enter Sky City. He described Acoma as "one of the strongest cities ever seen," because it was built on such a high cliff.

The day we were there, the women were baking bread, using a communal oven. It smelled so delicious. They had abundant supplies of maize, beans and turkeys, like those of New Spain. Some sat outside their adobe dwellings making exquisite pottery—beautifully designed in the warm earth colors of the Southwest. We purchased a water jug of very fine quality and then wished long afterward that we had bought several more.

By the following spring LaRue declared she was ready to come back to Kentucky. We fixed up a small studio on the grounds, with lots of windows for reading. As always, she embraced the change in her life's circumstances with considerable zest, contacting the county library for bookmobile services and writing to her grandchildren and friends back west. She was a fabulous pianist and was anxious for Buzz to develop into a fine musician. After she went back to Florida for the winter, she sent him scales to practice.

She still painted what she called her "bread and butter" oils and despite her age, turned them out rather quickly. But mostly she read and made hooked rugs and rag dolls. She did some light cooking or else took her meals at the Bar-B-Q ranch, and on occasion she ate dinner with us. She also accompanied me on my errands to town and, to my delight, was always ready to go with me whenever I went and entertained me with stories of her life. She talked about Iowa and her young days. I asked her once if she would ever go back, and she answered, "Why would I want to go back and look at barn roofs? Besides, I've outlived all of my friends." Although she was the same age as my grandmother, when I took her along to visit my mother and grandmother, she called them "the old ones."

One time I was driving down the mountains, returning from a buying trip on the reservation in Cherokee. It was hot, and I was exhausted. "I'm going to have a nervous breakdown," I declared. LaRue raised her voice in anger. "You are not going to have anything of the kind. Now, keep on driving."

Whenever we went out to dinner and finished our main course, the servers would ask if we'd like dessert. LaRue would respond the same way every time: "And what do you have?" Regardless of the offerings, she would move her chair, adjust her shoulders and say, "Make mine ice cream. I'm a descendent of Dolley Madison, you know." Her maiden name was Payne, so I suppose she might have been right.

She was anxious for me to travel and see other parts of the world. Once she said, "If you ever have any money, wear calico and travel. Don't go first class, either. You will be with people who have seen and done everything, and they're no fun. Stay with the young people. Then you will learn something. And be a collector. There will always be an element of excitement in your life."

She also told me one time, "If I'd had your looks and my brains…" knowing full well that she would not have changed anything about her own life. Of her sister, Pauline, she stated, "She can have her cherry furniture. I have my memories."

Indeed, it was talking about her life with Flaming Arrow that gave her the most pleasure.

James and I spent our first year of marriage in the tiny farming village of Acomita, sixty miles west of the Rio Grande River. Acomita (Little Acoma in Spanish) was where most of the Acomas went in the summer to raise their crops along the San Juan River, which would elsewhere be called a creek.

The main village of Acoma was about ten miles south, on a mesa three hundred feet high. A primitive road led to the top, on which sat a deep pool of rainwater, along with rock and adobe buildings. Some of the older ones extended three stories. Here on the Acoma Mesa, prehistoric people built a city out of rocks and mud. Many of the older houses were three stories. The windows were of gypsum rock slabs, which were opaque, admitting light. The lower rooms were for storing regalia and field crops.

The Mesa was flat on top, three hundred feet straight up from the valley floor. Built by nature, it was recognized as a safe place to hide from enemies. At the foot of the Mesa, in the time of the Spaniards a battle was fought. During the siege of their village, the

Acomas exhausted their store of arrows. So they caught bees and wasps from the crannies of the walls, put them in crockery jars and then dropped them down on the Spaniards below. This proved more effective than arrows. The Spaniards withdrew.

The Acomas still tell of several centuries of slavery and of carrying dirt up the steep walls in shawls on their backs to build an immense cathedral whose walls were seven feet thick. They also carried dirt to build a cemetery, forty feet deep, and the walls to enclose it.

There were many other big rocks of many shapes in the valley. One of immense size was later called the Enchanted Mesa, which was supposed to be the home of the gods. Some say that there was a village on top, but the Acomas deny this. Its walls are literally impossible to climb. Two men in all of history flew a kite with an attached rope across the top and made the ascent, but found no evidence that anyone had ever lived there. About a thousand people still live on top of Acoma, and the cathedral is still in use. The house walls are several feet thick. When one old house fell, a wall cavity was found filled with pinion nuts from centuries ago as a reserve for times of famine.

⤔

James and I moved into an adobe house and slept on the floor rolled in our blankets—decidedly romantic. We cooked in a fireplace, where fragrant pine wood both heated the room and flavored our food. In primitive days, heated stones were dropped into thick, clay pots to cook mush. In baskets made of rushes and lined with pinion pitch, food could be heated.

I liked the novelty, but did not like the mutton, which was our daily fare. I was sick for a while. The San Juan River was full of alkali and silt. James' mother made a paste of green juniper twigs and I ate it by the spoonful. Soon I could eat anything.

The snow was deep that winter on the Acoma Mesa, but we decided to go hunting for rabbits. My indulgent husband was not too enthusiastic, but the trip promised fresh meat, so we packed food in the back of our car and headed west into the forest and the hills.

We made a camp on the west side of the bluff near a big crack. A large pine had fallen, which assured plenty of wood for our fire. We would have slept well, but there was a cold wind blowing up the valley, and we were forced to get up often to replenish the fire.

This valley was covered by a sparse growth of bushy rabbit brush, pinion trees, a few mesquite bushes and juniper. The blue juniper berries still hung on the branches, so we picked a few to put in our stew. The wind increased. The boughs on the old pine trees creaked with each gust. The nighthawks darted in and out of the firelight. We made our bed in a crevice. Sleep was fitful, and extra pine limbs had to be added to the fire as it died down.

Morning came, clear and cold and creepy. Animal calls floated across the valley as we cooked our bacon and brewed our coffee. These were the voices of coyotes, echoed by the rock cliffs on both sides.

It sounded like hundreds of animals. Flaming Arrow told me that there were possibly only a few, but I was ready to give up the rabbit hunt. We packed the car to head for home. Taking my coat from a rock, I was amazed to see most of its fur collar in shreds. We had made our bed too close to the crevice, and in the night the pack rats that assembled their nests there had slipped down and carried off pieces. I had been so tired, and my sleep was so sound that they had nibbled around my neck without my noticing.

When we tried to start the car, it was frozen from the extreme cold. We spent the morning carrying red-hot coals, which we placed over and under the car at strategic places. We had to be careful not to melt the tires. At sunrise the coyote calls ceased. Flaming Arrow assured me that they never attacked—but when the car finally started, we were glad to leave. When we arrived home, we found the snow had drifted up to our window sills.

We had plenty of mutton, along with homegrown wheat bread baked in round loaves in the beehive adobe ovens outside. There was a long trough divided into large, black lava slab compartments, all rough and of different textures. Wheat or shelled corn was taken through each section and rubbed on the rock, ground into coarse or fine flour as desired. The prehistoric Acomas dug holes in the rocks at the bases of the cliffs for this purpose, and many of these grinding pits can be seen to this day.

All twenty-two Pueblo villages lying along the Rio Grande River had dancers who performed seasonally. Because they celebrated incidents from the Pueblos' religious history, the dancers were masked, and only Indians were permitted to watch them.

Their deerskin masks were made inside the Kivas, the underground ceremonial chambers. The first coat of color was white or turquoise, the white being a gypsum paint, the blue from copper rocks from the valley below. Black was made from the gum of the bee-gum plant—ground fine, then boiled until it settled to the bottom as a thick, black paste. It was also used to decorate pottery. Paint was taken into the mouth and then blown onto the masks. Bold designs were applied with a chewed brush made from yucca stems. Next, a wide band of cedar branches and freshly gathered flowers was placed around the dancers' shoulders and decorated with eagle or hawk feathers—never owl.

Their arms were bare. On their elbows were pine branches, and at their waists were homespun aprons of white with black, red and green yarn embroidery—never blue. Painted gourd rattles were held in both hands. Drummers were seated on the dirt. Choir singers stood at one side. Their songs told of the ancient dancers who came from Wee-Nee-Nah, their prehistoric tribal abode.

According to legend, these dancers were not originally masked. They were feasted by the villagers to whom they brought gifts of food. But there were some ugly ones among them, and on one occasion the Acomas made fun of their big noses and homely faces, not knowing they were gods and could understand their words. So the next time they arrived masked and fought the Acomas—and then stopped coming with their generous gifts.

Dances celebrated the native seasons, such as rains, corn planting and the harvest. On this day Flaming Arrow and I had driven into the village of Zuni, one of the Pueblos, for a pair of moccasins. We heard the drums, and the Zunis were dancing in the plaza, the open courtyard of the houses. He cautioned me that they were having a masked dance, and that I was not to look too long at the dancers, but to turn and gaze at the mountains from time to time.

We climbed a ladder to a second-story rooftop. The edges of the roofs around the plaza were filled with Pueblo spectators. The dancers' costumes were exceedingly colorful, and whole animal skins hung behind their waists, the tails dragging the ground.

Zuni men wore black shawls and black broad-brimmed felt hats drawn down over their eyes. The men would approach me, almost touching my face, with their blankets pulled around their faces. Huge earrings with turquoise pendants hung from their earlobes. I would smile, and they would walk away. Flaming Arrow said they had caught on that I had seen the masked dancers at Acoma.

We took a hurried leave. This incident created much trouble in Acoma. The elders debated as to what they should do to get me out of the village. Their drums beat on the night air as they argued. I was totally unaware of any danger, until one morning I had a caller, a middle-aged man who spoke English.

He informed me that under no circumstances was I to go to Acoma when the masked dances were in progress. I saw right then and there that if I showed the least bit of fear, I was lost. So I told him, "Now, see here! I was married to James by a white judge, and I have a right to go anywhere in the Pueblo that other wives go. If I want to, I will come up into one of the dances and sit down on the ground in the center. Yes, you might kill me, but do you know what will happen then? When my daughter hears about it, she will go straight to Washington, and they will send soldiers and take all of the Acomas and put them in prison like they did Geronimo—and that will be the last dance you will ever have."

They knew about Fort Sill prison. That was the last I heard on the subject. Fortunately I did not need to carry out my threat, for soon afterward we received a letter from the Swarthmore Chautauquas, inviting us to do program work. We took three other Indians with us. One was a young man who couldn't sing, but who looked typically Indian. We pieced out his costume with leftovers from ours. When we were asked about his tribe, we made up a name.

⚅

We drove to the Conchiti Pueblo village and watched the natives dance the rain down from the clouds. Dancers formed groups of men and women, and then made a long line in the plaza. Small boys and girls were at the end of the line, all in costume. The women danced barefoot, with wooden tablets on their heads. The men wore eagle feathers in their hair, pinion and juniper branches on their elbows and paint on their faces and bodies. Intertwined among them danced the "ghosts," coated gray with ashes, representing the spirits of the Ancient Ones, still among them but unseen. Rain clouds gathered slowly in the east, but finally commenced in a deluge. Soaking wet, the Indians continued dancing and singing.

One night, in Santa Domingo Pueblo, with my bed of blankets against the wall and about ten Domingo men and my husband seated before the fireplace on the floor, we exchanged tribal songs. Their drum beat so softly that I soon fell asleep to their music. In the morning we were served breakfast, tiny fish which looked like sardines, caught from the Rio Grande River and prepared especially for us. The Pueblos have a superstition about fish; they will not eat them. As we left, the men lined up outside the door, their blankets as colorful as bright flowers in the fall morning sunshine.

At Christmastime we drove again up the Rio Grande Valley to Santa Domingo. As we called on special friends, we saw a Christmas tree in each home, beautiful pines that reached to ceiling, all elaborately decorated with tinsel and glass balls. On the walls were pictures of saints.

After a supper of mutton stew, we waited for the entertainers. It was their custom for individual groups to go from house to house and entertain with their stunts. There were fine dancers in elaborate costumes, singers with new songs composed for the season, and jokes bandied about incidents that were supposed to be secret.

At one point, three very fat men, naked except for their G-strings, came in, bent over the fire in the fireplace, lit their corn husk cigarettes and then walked out without saying a word.

Another year, while on the Acoma Mesa, we sat on the wall on the east side and watched various dancing groups enter and leave the church and parade through the streets, with drums beating and singers singing. There was a bright yellow moon that night. It rose over the Enchanted Mesa in the distance—an unforgettable sight.

⊸⊱

Flaming Arrow had spoken of the caves in the lava beds. New Mexico had many extinct volcanoes, where cones and their hardened lava flows were a distinct part of the scenery. About sixty miles west of the Rio Grande and then about sixty miles south were two. The lava, black and porous, had flowed northward for many miles and formed a streak about five miles wide. Its swirls had sharp ridges, and large and small caves could be found throughout. The caves were the homes of many wild animals, particularly mountain lions and bobcats. There were also ancient storage caves containing masks and pottery. But the lava ridges were like knife blades, making walking very difficult.

We decided to make a trip there to find these relics. We took an Indian named Wee-Mah along, as he knew the locations, south of the north road from Gallup. We soon passed the big spring of the old Indian Village of San Rafael. These villages had Spanish names given them by the Conquistadors, as do the mountains. That village was only a small group of adobe houses and a Spanish church where the penitents held their eastern Crucifixion rites.

We left the car and walked along the stretch of lava. There in a cave we found four full-grown sheep that were strays, having been born there and belonging to no one. Wee-Mah could not resist adding the four to his flock. He crowded them into the back of his car and insisted on going right home. There was no room left for me. We had a small dog with us, so Flaming Arrow asked if I would be willing to stay in a big cave on a neighboring bluff. He placed our bedding inside, and we gathered wood for a fire, enough to keep all night. Off the two men drove to Acoma, twenty miles away.

I wasn't afraid until dark, when two huge owls began to hoot with big bass voices. Their nest was in a hole in a rock right above the cave. Then a dark cloud gathered in the west with vivid lightning and then loud thunder. I retired as far back inside as I could drag my bedding. The little dog whined. Rain pelted down over the mouth of the cave, and I had to drag the bedding back still farther. I could not move the fire, so the blazes and embers died out.

At last the sun rose over the Mesa, and at long last Flaming Arrow returned, having driven all night in the mud. This episode much increased my reputation among the Acomas as "The Woman Afraid of Nothing."

⤙

Flaming Arrow had an uncle in the Pueblo who was offered a lecture program in the East. We were invited to join the group, so we went to Kansas City and gave programs from there. There we met noted Indian tenor Chief Silver Tongue, who wanted all of us to join him at the opening of the new Opera House in Springfield, Missouri. We created a stage backdrop. I wore a buckskin dress, a black wig with long braids and lots of face paint and beads. Silver Tongue sang the Indian Love Call to me from the balcony and then came on the stage and sang.

The lure of the footlights drew us. I'd had years of experience presenting programs with public school students. So I asked myself, "Why not gather our own Indian talent and book ourselves in the eastern states?"

We wrote the Indian School in Haskell, Kansas, and they sent us another Sioux, an extremely handsome lad with a fine tenor voice. My own pupil from the Pueblo and my husband practiced daily. I wrote to the most noted Chautauqua in the East—the Swarthmores. They had been searching for an Indian group, but since they had not yet heard us, if we would come to them and they liked us, they would contract us. On that slim promise and at our own expense, we drove east by way of Wisconsin Dells, where our new friend Chief Silver Tongue was the headliner in a summer pageant comprised entirely of Indians from many tribes.

Here my Indians got valuable experience in pleasing audiences. We were accepted by the Swarthmores and given a limousine for travel. We were with them for two seasons. From then on my life was occupied with programs for many years.

We also spent one year in Ecuador, South America, where Flaming Arrow made two trips into the Amazon jungles, gathering words of the various indigenous languages, endeavoring to make a comparison with his own Pueblo, as he was alleged to have descended from either the Incas or the Aztecs.

She and Flaming Arrow had met many people, but Ernest Thompson

Seton, who held international fame as a wildlife artist and storyteller, was a special friend. She talked about him and his wife with admiration. She also spoke proudly of her three granddaughters, Barbara, Betty and Martha, all professional women. When Martha, a schoolteacher, met and married a Navajo, LaRue was ecstatic. "At last," she said, "I have an Indian in my family."

One late afternoon she went blackberry picking along the edge of the highway below her cabin. Beyond the view of passersby, she slipped and fell beneath the bank. Unable to climb out, she made herself as comfortable as possible among the brambles and then lay there all night long. A cry for help would have been futile with the highway traffic. So she just waited for morning.

Arising early, Carlo saw her light still shining in the window. He became alarmed and raced to her house, only to find her gone. In a panic, he ran along the highway, calling her name. For a few minutes all was quiet, but soon he heard her voice. He lifted her, carried her home and then commanded her to see a doctor.

I sat in Dr. Griffith's waiting room—and waited and waited, fearing the worst. All of a sudden, LaRue walked through the examining room door with a weary exhilaration in her voice: "That interesting man. I don't know when I've had such a good conversation." I asked her if she was all right. She answered, "Of course I am."

After one summer and fall here at the village, LaRue was ready to travel farther south for the winter. She went to Bryson City, North Carolina. She planned to come back the following year. All of her letters to us carried her strong, unique, stylistic voice.

1967

My dearly Loved Lucille,

   I cannot begin to tell you how I value your letters. I sit out every day with my paintings, and I do like it so well here. My landlord is a gangling redhead, half toothless (as most everyone down here is from snuff using). Their toothless grins get my goat. My landlord's wife comes to see me often. They own about half of this section. She's planning on going to Florida for a month or two to stock up with tarpon shells for crafts that she plans on making. So now, my dear, do not worry about me anymore. I'm in a good place and with good people.

⚜

Carlo has always been kind to me. I do not know how to express myself to him, but I feel so grateful to him for everything. Lucille, you have met your trials head on, and still you have taken time to do for me. I can truly say that you and your family have been dearer to me than anyone on earth.

She had met Gene and Louie, who were part-Indian, and their wives Thelma and Sally here at the village. They had moved to Tennessee for the winter, but visited LaRue in North Carolina.

Louie gave me a beautiful box of paints someone gave him. Also, Thelma and Sally gave me seven jars apiece of canned goods and a lovely comforter. The poor always have something to give. Another rainy morning just began, but I have orders ahead, although the weatherman says, "Rain through the middle of September." Let it rain, let it pour, there ain't no rain where I'm headed for.

⚜

My dear substitute daughter,
I'm so glad you asked me to help Carcille with her essay. It will prove I am not senile or weak-minded yet, if they take that attitude. Write me at your leisure (if you have any).

Determined to go to Florida for the winter, she dickered with some folks in Ft. Pierce about transforming a small garage into an artist's studio.

Your letters were so inquiring, thanks a million. I'm not too well, but I'm going to be all right. I do lots of reading and a little painting. No news, of course. Write me when you can. You are as dear to me as a real relative, and then some.

Concerned about Interstate 75 bypassing our village, she searched for a new location for us. Trailer parks were new and hot. Perhaps we'd be interested.

Talked with a big motel owner who said this is a very poor tourist season. They have house cars parking in the trailer parks. Tell Carlo to be very leery of anything but trailer camps. Put in lights and toilet, but no cabins. This is still going to be a good campsite here. The new freeway will go around Bryson City, Andrews & Murphy. The outlet is very close here. I can see it, about 200 feet away. My landlord plans to sell this location for a motel, not my location, but close. You could lease this, keep your lovely home, just another of my ideas, which I do not charge you for. Ha ha. After my two good summers' trade, it is baffling to do nothing. Oh well, such is life. As long as I am well, I am in luck.

After consideration and with too much rainfall, she began thinking about going to an Eastern Star Home.

My dear Lucille,
Drip, drip, drip. The rains come dripping. Can you hear them? Yes, yes, yes. Please have Mr. Mounts send in my application for the Masonic Home as soon as possible.
Additional data:
My father Dillon Payne was a knight templar of Bloomfield, IA. He was an attorney there for 60+ years. Oh yes, mayonnaise is fine cold cream. I read it in a magazine and am trying it. Works fine. Beats Jergens.

The heavy rainfall that kept coming clouded her sunshine for a good season. Her paintings were her consuming interest. I supplied the panels for her work.

I am so well, except for my usual accidents. Dropped a chair on my leg and gouged out a hunk. When I don't hear from you, I think you are sick.

This letter arrived in response to my daughter Betsy.

My dear little sugar lump,
Your Cherokee card brightened the day for me when it came. I love to be remembered by the Fort Sequoyah clan and to see I am

not forgotten by you. You have very pretty handwriting. Be a good girl and study hard, especially that new method math which is too hard for me.

⌁

Nothing to add. Still looks like rain. I am painting today. Have you any plans on a new location? The four-lane highway will begin here. It will go right past my door here, so I'd better hang onto this a little longer. Love to you all. Do write, or one of your many children can.

My little sugar lump's card was so appreciated.

Back in Cottonwood, Arizona, once more, LaRue settled herself into the comforts of her granddaughter Barbara's house. The highway had taken her little house in Bryson City, and it was time to touch base with her family.

My dear Carloftis family,

How glad I am to have food and shelter in these terrible times. We are in the lull of a snow storm with another due this afternoon. The snow is over four feet deep, no drifty winds, so this is the level. The snow is up to my waist. No record of such a snow. Hundreds of tourists are marooned in motels, hotels, private homes. Families around Flagstaff advised to buy two weeks' food. Helicopter dropping hay to Navajo cattle and sheep. Barbara is working at the hospital, not only her shift, but for nurses snowed in at Jerome. The next storm almost as bad. It makes me think of Iowa when I was young.

Disappointed at losing her Bryson City house, she was looking into coming back to North Carolina, preferably somewhere along U.S. Highway 19, where the tourist trade was. Jerome was a copper ghost town.

I can't do anything but dream in this weather, so here are some of my dreams. You have a beautiful high soprano voice. What the others have, tell me each by name. Then why not a Carloftis trio or

*quartet. Buzz can plan each part for them. You have fine ones I got
for you. "Lift thine eyes," "The red, red rose," the first to learn.
Let Betsy and Koula on one part, when you get your part, Buzz can
be the piano soloist, so he should have another one and keep up
the one he was on. I was so happy over the snapshots you sent me.
I have a pendant for Betsy. It has copper from the Jerome Copper.
Sorry it isn't as valuable as Koula's, but a different one. I will send
it when the mail clears up, too crowded now.*

⤫

*My very dear family,
    This is a beautiful day. Not a cloud in the sky. I saw the
weather section and greatly fear you have snow and that I picked
out a good week to be here. The little towns in New Mexico and
Arizona along with trips have grown so. I can hardly accept the
changes. Tucson is now 350,000. I have been chasing around
once at a Chinese restaurant where I had endive salad, etc. Last
Saturday we drove to Nogales, Mexico, and had a good time, four
of us. I wanted to buy everything.*

She was reminded of the first atom bomb at Trinity, New Mexico.
She was in Albuquerque when a rancher came to the curio shop and said
he was ordered to round up his cattle and move them. He couldn't, and
the hair on their backs turned white. He said they had gone somewhere
for testing. Another letter from Arizona:

*I am still concerned about Carlo's foot. When you write, be
sure to tell me. Tell the children that we have three big German
police dogs here. One is the biggest dog I ever saw and beautifully
marked. They are gentle. I miss the children very much. They are
good children, though loud at times. Ha ha. The trip to Nogales
was tiered with mountains. I am well and at work with my paints
and panels. Take care of your health.*

She returned from Arizona to Ft. Pierce, Florida, for the winter.
Shortly after she got settled in her apartment, LaRue began looking
again for a business location for us.

My dear Lucille,

So very glad to year from you. Here are further things for you to ponder. There is no tourist trade in Ft. Pierce. Sebring is cut off from main travel. The trade like you have will concentrate around the Disney Area, which will have curio shops, already signed up for. Mrs. Foder, who has made herself rich, talked with me. She says your six children will prevent you from leasing a shop or motel, children a burden here.

❧

Dear Lucille,

I am so sick these last two days. Being treated here at Hill Haven. Will not come to Kentucky in March. I'd better stay here and get treated. An infection, sick stomach, head and backache. Counting on you for final help as per letter if end comes. So sick.

❧

1970

Fearing the strike might affect us, I call this your Christmas letter. The Harbor House sold and now is being torn down. We all had to move at once. My Harbor House family moved over here to this country home, and I have been so disgusted and upset. It is expensive but nice, $69 a month, but so institutional. I have my three big boxes of stuff stored in the basement, and here I sit, mad as a wet hen, not allowed to do anything. The food is fine, but the inmates, walking ghosts or worse. I have about the only roommate that is okay, but she bosses me around, rather hard to take, but I read a lot and sew a little. I'm planning on a shop and have a mail carrier out of Murphy, North Carolina, scouting. I am not happy in institutional life. I get hungry for fried onions.

Love to my lovely family in Kentucky.

❧

I am well —well enough. I have just been playing piano for a bunch of derelicts right after breakfast, <u>by request.</u> Poor things, just derelicts. I guess I am one, too.

I have a nice room and a good roommate, my age, and a Puritan if ever there was one. A niece of Henry Ward Bucker, an old maid. Takes a bath every night.

⌘

This is a bitter cold morning. I will have to go out for meals, but dread it. The next time you come to Florida, I will give you the Navajo saddle blanket for Dusty. It has a small history. It is said to be the finest ever made by the Navajos and was given to me by a Navajo boy in Laguna, and I promised never to sell it. I know Dustan will treasure it.

⌘

1971
Your letter was like a tonic. Everything about everybody. What a family you have. Such talent, such good looks. Just watch Dusty.

She then moved closer to her granddaughter, Barbara, who was a nurse at the local hospital. Barbara visited often, doing her laundry and shopping.

1972
Write the Copper Hill Firm and ask them if they are interested in copper in another location. It would be close to haul. If they are, don't tell them where it is, but go lease it for 10 years. Lease it from owner and sublease it to the Copper Hill Firm. Barbara is head nurse at the hospital where I stayed a week with a hurt knee, otherwise I am well, only beginning to feel my age. (Isn't 93 awful?) Also, tell Koula to cut out from magazines and papers the heads for a scrapbook of hairdos.

⌘

My dear dear Carloftises, one and all,
If my body could fly as fast as my thoughts do, I would be with

all of you often. I have fine health. Soon I'll be 95. Horrors! I'm in my little home among the big cottonwood trees. And people move in and out. Some nice and some not. Barbara, my granddaughter, comes every other day, and we shop in a big store. I get SS check, so I am blessed in my old age. My cat is a very long-haired calico. I had it altered. Drowning kittens is too much for me.

Kiss yourselves mentally for me.

❧

My dear Lucille and family,

My long delayed letter to you is actually started. I've been invited out to dinner, and I go to Service each Sunday, and Barbara buys my groceries. I haven't much to tell you, except do let me hear from you often. Your gifts have enabled me to dress well. I sleep well and eat better. I try to paint poorly. My friends are boring. I guess I'm rich and don't know it. At any rate, the bankers aren't going to Europe on my money.

❧

This is a small, long drawn-out town. My sprained knee is keeping me in a lot. I am afraid of falling, but by spring, I will be normal. I hope you will visit me anytime, and in the meantime, the Lord be with you and yours and keep you all well. I love you all. Write when you can, and when you can't, have Betsy, who does a mighty fine job.

Thanks a million for the box. Barbara's eyes bugged out when she saw the dress.

❧

1974
My dear Mrs. Carloftis,

I am sorry I was unable to write to you. I couldn't find your address anywhere. My grandmother died last April. She died very suddenly and had been in good health until then. I want to thank you for your many kindnesses to her. She was so fond of you all. I *am returning your package, and please forgive me for not writing sooner.*

Sincerely,
Barbara Jones

When I received the note, I read it once, then tucked it into my jacket pocket. Later in the day, I told my family the sad news. A year passed. One day I put my hand inside that same jacket pocket and was surprised to find the letter still there.

Rockcastle Queen

The Travel Bus

The approach of the winter holidays had obviously been on Carlo's mind, because late one afternoon in 1965, I heard air brakes outside the store go, "Swooshie." A bus door flew open, and out bolted Carlo. I looked for the driver, but there was no one sitting in the front seat. I peered inside. No one was inside the twenty-four seater, either. I could tell Carlo was enjoying a moment of excitement. He had been talking about buying a bus someday and converting it into a travel home. But it had to be a Flexible, he said—sharp and streamlined.

I shrugged and walked slowly back inside the store. I should have known by now that with his rolled brim hat, his black leather vest, bolo tie and Justin boots, when Carlo set his heart on something, he wouldn't rest until he got it.

The bus had been on a run from Somerset to Nashville, and it would be an ideal way for our family to travel. No more, "Sorry, we are full" when motel managers counted heads—or making a price prohibitive when we inquired about a month or longer stay. No more standing in line at public restrooms. No more trailers whipping us around in the wind. We could prepare our own meals, sleep in our own beds. The children could get up, move and play. This would be our home away from home.

It all sounded so agreeable and actually made a lot of sense—but still, it was hard for me to accept. The next morning Carlo settled the deal, and after a very restless night I went to see a doctor. I told him about Carlo's new bus. There was nothing physically wrong with me, he said, except that I needed to calm down.

Now that the bus had become a reality, we were in a hurry to get it converted into proper living quarters. So we took it to a trailer factory in Indiana and then rode the ferry across the Ohio River to the historic town of Vevey. We hoped it would be finished for the Christmas holidays.

Motor homes at that time were fairly new, and we had only seen one before—in South Florida. It had a kitchen, breakfast nook, full bath and bunk beds. Its cinnamon and cream sofa fabric had a nubby finish. The handsome exterior was painted light beige and trimmed in wide silver panels, extending its full length. We thought it worthy of the highway and were anxious to get going.

When we went to pick it up, our car was packed tight with children, including one little friend who had begged to come along. When they saw it, all gleaming and ready to roll, they could hardly contain themselves.

Carlo backed it out of the lot, and then, with great ceremony, pulled onto the highway, all seven children in tow. I followed behind in our car. Carlo nearly slipped over the bank once, but from there the ride was smooth. When we got back to Livingston, everyone wanted to blow the horn.

There was plenty of storage, so I packed everything, too much, really. For someone who'd had her doubts about the whole bus idea, I was beginning to feel a flurry of excitement and was eager to embark upon our journey.

One by one our children climbed inside, each carrying his or her favorite toy, or whatever they were attached to at the moment, and sat down. All was quiet now, but I could tell by their expressions that they couldn't wait to get moving.

Ruby LeFevers, our longtime friend from Pineville, who had been working with us at the village for years, stepped inside to see us off. "Look," I said. "I just know these are the cutest children I have ever seen." She responded, "You won't know one from the other by the time you get home."

We crossed the Rockcastle River and headed south. Our first trip! This was such a new traveling concept that wherever we stopped, people would gather, and some would even ask to look inside. Once I overheard someone calling our bus a land yacht.

Over the next few months, whenever we weren't on the road, the bus became the children's playhouse. When school let out for winter break, we headed to Florida and hit the beaches.

Leaving Kentucky one cold, snowy morning, instead of driving down the east coast, we decided to go through Tallahassee. We loved taking different routes and seeing brand-new countryside. It often stimulated us to the point that we were already planning another trip before we had reached the destination of our current one.

Unfortunately, just as we were about to pull into Tallahassee, the bus stopped dead—luckily, right near a service station. This was, of course, before the days of car and cell phones. After a quick check, a mechanic determined that we needed a new part. But there was none available except from the Flexible manufacturer in Loudinville, Ohio.

There was nothing for us to do but wait. Our salvation was the animal clinic lot across the street. For four days we stayed parked, awaiting shipment, and for four days we took walks, read books, played rummy and board games and ate our friend Janie's Christmas fruitcake, which I had thankfully thought to bring along. Buzz and Dusty spent a lot of time sitting on the curb, watching ladies bring in poodles wearing fancy jeweled collars. They rolled their eyes, thinking, I'm sure, of their far less pampered country dogs back home.

When we were finally ready to leave, I asked if the children could tour the animal hospital. Permission granted. They took their time walking through, enjoying it very much—a good way, I thought, to end four days of being stranded by the side of the road.

The stopover had been a luxury, actually, and when we arrived in Florida, we soaked up plenty of sunshine, played in the ocean, ate fresh caught fish dinners and were saved from the temptation of staying a little bit longer and missing school.

But more things began going wrong with the bus. The heater, for example. It was comfortable in the daytime, but the nights were freezing. Now I was definitely ready to go home. I was tired of going to bed wearing my hat.

On our way back north, we noticed a drive-in theater and decided that a good movie would have a calming influence on us both. But first we had to find a trailer park and reserve a space for the night. That settled, we drove several miles back south and saw a wonderful production, ate plenty of popcorn and drank Cokes.

It was well past midnight when we got back to the park, decorated with a tiny string of lights out front. We pulled in, and Carlo slowly backed into our designated space. But the gears got stuck in reverse, so instead of going forward, we kept rolling backward. This went on and on until the park lights were barely visible. Finally, Carlo gave up, shut off the motor, and we went to bed.

The next morning we looked outside and caught sight of a man sitting on a red tractor. He was waving his arms, calling out to us, "Merry Christmas!" We were sitting in the middle of a cotton field.

Undaunted, when the time came for another school break, we hit the road again, this time to the Smoky Mountains and into Cherokee. We bought merchandise for our store, and as always, had fun. Then we headed back across the mountain. Coming down the steep Tennessee side, the engine died. Carlo had apparently used the brakes so much, that the flag dropped in front of his face reading, "Low pressure." He calmly put on the emergency brakes and maneuvered the bus to the shoulder, where we finally came to a complete stop.

By then black smoke was billowing up from the wheels. The door flew open, and everyone jumped out. I grabbed Jon and my purse and followed my family to safety as fast as I could. The children were already scampering over a hill to find water. I just stood there with a baby in my arms and wished the darn thing would burn to the ground. After the brakes cooled, though, we were on our way again and got home without anymore trouble.

For weeks afterward, the bus sat proudly in front of our house. Late one evening after we had closed the store, I looked out and saw three men dressed in suits walking all around it, looking it over as they talked. They backed up and took longer views, still talking. Finally, one yelled toward the house. I went to the door. They inquired about who owned it and if it were for sale. I told them that I didn't think so; it belonged to my husband, who was away.

They replied that they were the Don Reno Brothers on their way to Cincinnati to star on the Porter Waggoner Show. I half believed them. We were so isolated, though, that when night came, I began to feel afraid. How silly I had been to tell those men that Carlo wasn't there! I pulled down a .22 rifle from the wall and waited. The next evening I was watching the Porter Waggoner Show, and sure enough, the same three men were introduced.

Ruby looked up from where she was sitting, puffing on her cigarette and calmly asked, "Are those the fellows you drawed the gun on last night?"

Buzz later drove the bus on its last trip to Florida and then parked it in a trailer park. We visited it once or twice more. And then we sold it.

St. Augustine In A Beetle Buy

We were getting ready to take our annual Christmas break, and our bags, with flower-power daisies pasted all over them, were packed. The children were teenagers now, with the exceptions of Dusty, who was seven, and Jon, who was two. Carlo and I were looking forward to the usual traveling "pile up."

Our children, so wholesome in both attitude and effort, all smart, with the older ones already armed with awards and distinctions, had brought us so much pleasure. Our lives were simply jam-packed with church, club and school activities—Bible school, girls auxiliary, church camp, football and basketball practices, cheerleading, band, weightlifting, incessant efforts to tone their bodies to build muscles or enter beauty pageants.

But early one morning we walked up toward the store and found that it had been broken into and robbed. Our car had been stolen.

We nearly went into shock. Then we collapsed. But not for long. We had another smaller car, a turquoise Volkswagen convertible with a black canvas top. We held a family powwow. If we took our planned vacation trip, we probably would not be able to buy another car anytime soon. We left the decision up to them.

Suitcases were quickly unpacked, and our things were crammed into small bundles. There would be no fancy dress-up dinners this time. There was no space for anything except bathing suits, short sets and underwear. Somehow we managed to pack enough clothing for seven people in that tiny trunk and then drove away, giggling.

There was no room for Buzz, age fifteen, and I suspected that he was happier that there wasn't. Our three daughters squeezed into the back seat, and Dusty sat in the hole behind them where the top rested when rolled back. I held Jon on my lap. Sometimes he would lie across his sisters' laps. They never minded holding him; they all adored him.

We stopped every fifty miles or so to stretch our legs. As we all piled out of that tiny car, people began pointing and staring. Koula got embarrassed and refused to move.

We arrived at our favorite motel in St. Augustine in record time. The doors flew open, and we simply poured out, tired but glad we had made it. Koula emerged, swollen and stiff-legged.

We zipped all over town, ate at our favorite restaurants, walked and sunbathed on the beach, built sand castles and watched the seagulls as they trod the water waiting for food before being swept away with the next tide. When the week finally ended, and we got back home, we all agreed that we'd had a wonderful time.

But before going inside, we took a snapshot of our family standing in front of that Volkswagen, piled high with all of our belongings. Somehow we had found room for a steam iron, a bag of oranges—and enough happy memories to last a lifetime.

Over the years we continued to make trips to St. Augustine, our beloved home away from home. By the late 1970s Carlo and I had visited most of the city's romantic attractions. But the children had not. One year, after some discussion, they decided they should tour Potter's Wax Museum. Carlo and I sat across the street and relaxed, drinking coffee and Cokes, listening to the rhythm of the horses' hooves as they gently pulled sightseeing carriages along the cobblestones.

An hour passed, then two. We waited and waited. Finally we strolled over to the museum to see how much longer the children would be. To our surprise we found Koula lying in repose on a fainting sofa, her brothers and sisters gathered around her in attendance.

Back in the car, Jon's mind was apparently still fixated on the maladies of King Henry VIII. At age fourteen, Jon had shot up so fast that summer that we had hardly noticed. But all at once he held up both hands and cried out, "Look, Daddy, look at my hands. I've got the gout––and nobody cares!"

Carlo calmly reassured him that there was nothing to worry about. He had just hit a growth spurt. Soon we were all back at the beach, quite happily running and playing against the waves.

I-75 Changes Our Lives

*O*ur parking lot, once filled with cars, was now empty, and the beat of the rawhide drum was fast becoming a distant memory. Overnight, our business at Fort Sequoyah had dwindled to just a few customers per day. By 1969, Interstate 75 had opened, and we were now far off the beaten path. No more steady traffic. All of the Indians had returned earlier to the reservation, except for Lightfoot. He stayed on for several more years, but eventually he too was gone.

We began trying to rebuild our lives. Grateful that most of our children were now grown or away at college, with only Dusty and Jon still at home, Carlo and I took walks in the woods and canoe trips down the river. We shopped for a new car and read books. We thought about our friends from Canada who had suddenly lost their jobs. Instead of moping around, feeling sorry for themselves, they'd packed a few things in their shiny red Thunderbird and headed to New Orleans for a week.

So we joined the crowds at Pigeon Forge and Gatlinburg, Tennessee, with the backdrop of the beautiful Smoky Mountains, in search of a suitable alternate location. But we resisted any thoughts of moving away from the river and uprooting our family. Eventually we just settled down and decided to live on a reduced income.

The store was still operating at a low volume, but that gave us scant comfort. We had to cut, cut, cut—until finally it was apparent that we needed to make a choice. We were not ready to retire; we still wanted to work. And we were reminded of a friend from Cherokee who'd retired and gone to Florida. He confessed that the first thing he did was buy an easy chair. Then he went to the library and checked out stacks of books. His romantic dream of leisure, however, didn't last long. We hardly had time to miss him before he was back from the sunny south and in business once again.

We searched our minds for something that might work better. After all, we'd operated a fine business here for many years, and we knew that our customers were still traveling—for the most part, down I-75. With highway signs and brochures, perhaps we could capture their attention once again without too much financial risk. Attractions were springing up across the country, drawing capacity crowds. More and more people were driving south, and they wanted to be entertained.

As it turned out, we still couldn't find any place that we liked better than right on the river. Satisfied that we had made the decision to stay, we hired an architect to draw up the new plan we had in mind: a miniaturized riverboat town, typical of the early nineteenth century, complete with a bank, hotel, telegraph office, blacksmith's shop, livery stable, doctor's office, printing press, grocery and feed store, school house, post office, even a theater with café tables and chairs for live stage shows. We knew we could pull it all together. Again, the location was perfect, and the theme would be easy to create, with a paddle-wheeler for cruises and a horse-drawn surrey. There was nothing like this in our area. We could offer lectures regarding the well-documented events of Camp Wildcat and of the river's importance to this Civil War battle. And about earlier times, when the river was used to float timber, furs, mountain herbs and other commodities. On special occasions, maybe we'd even hire a banjo player.

It all sounded so good. We were desperate to get our business going again. We'd missed the excitement of buying, selling and meeting new people. The valley was suddenly alive once more with furious hammering and sawing. Carlo was in charge of the construction, and he wasted no time on particulars. That was my job. I was to furnish these small structures in the appropriate fashions of the era. I got so caught up in the activity and purpose of it all, that it was like building a playhouse. Then I remembered that this was serious business, and that I shouldn't go overboard with needless spending. So I shopped antique stores and close-outs for fixtures and trappings that would provide the proper ambiance.

Luckily, I found most of the furnishings right here in our county. Old book cabinets, school desks and blackboards, a giant mirror, a marble counter and other drugstore memorabilia, tools for the blacksmith's shop, and a telephone switchboard that was still in use when we came here. And as always, there was the natural landscape of trees and beautiful wild plants that gave us daily pleasures. A local art student sculpted the heads of mannequins into the style befitting their place of residence. I shopped vintage stores for clothing and studied old photos from museums. And whenever I felt pangs of uncertainty, I began sweeping the rough boardwalks. By the time we were finished, the broom was worn down to its handle.

The post office was the only authentic building. Rough and hewn, it was built in 1916 by my great uncle Morgan and was moved from its location, some thirty miles north of the river. Still intact were the numbered mailboxes, a bench, old posters and the small potbellied stove that I had warmed myself by as a child. Street lamps, special-ordered, completed the scene.

The Palace saloon looked like something straight out of an old Wild West movie set—with red flocked wallpaper, a long wooden counter with a huge lighted mirror behind it, a player piano and a dazzling crystal chandelier. Gunfighters and cancan dancers brought everything to life. A smart and talented Dixieland band, with young boys dressed in striped shirts and white trousers and straw Panama hats, entertained crowds. Outside, tourists strolled down to the river to cruise on the Rockcastle Queen.

We'd had the boat built in eastern Tennessee, and press releases were distributed to the towns it would pass by before arriving here. This replica paddle-wheeler seating twenty-eight passengers was a dream, with its turned posts and finials, all painted white. The seats were a shiny bright red, with life jackets stacked beneath. It was quite the beauty, and we were delighted with it.

There was little fanfare, though, when it was launched. The fresh, outdoor smell of the river filled our nostrils as the wheel gently turned and splashed. It had a majestic look moored alongside the lush, flowering riverbank. The path followed and crossed a part of Wilderness Road, where early settlers had forged the river and blazed the cane thickets. That was an adventure in itself, as we stepped down into the coolness and shade from the overhanging tree branches—another world down there, known only to the raccoons, ducks, canoeists and fishermen.

What we didn't realize was that the season would be so short, three months maximum. If it rained a lot, the river was turbulent and unsafe. If it were a dry spell, there were places too shallow to navigate. During good times, the boat was usually filled to delightful capacity. But at the end of most days, we didn't have a lot of interesting things to talk about. Life was suddenly dull.

So this too was a short-lived venture. After only three seasons we closed the town. We were unable to capture the spirit of America's traveler. Through no deliberate intention of our customers, they could not find us, tucked away on the river, yet so close to the exit that was still undeveloped forest land.

We continued on with our store, but the town that was once lively was now a mere museum designed for quiet walks. And then finally, land on the exit opened for private ownership. We had been wishing this would happen—so Carlo traded several hundred acres bounded by the national forest. Money could not buy this exit tract. It was land for land.

A renewed excitement and enthusiasm came upon us, and we built a new store on the property's south corner. In keeping with early-style architecture, the building was rustic, with a wood shake roof and a sweeping front porch. A huge water wheel was on one end, and it turned and splashed rhythmically. The store was furnished with our brand of merchandise, looking similar to the one we'd left behind.

But tourists moved hurriedly in and out of the establishment, looking more for a place to eat than for the beautiful gifts that we offered. For most, I-75 was a destination trip. People were no longer willing to stop someplace for an hour or so of sightseeing or the shopping pleasures we once knew on U.S. Highway 25. Everyone was now in such a hurry. They paused just long enough to fill up their gas tanks and grab a quick lunch.

We soon realized that this wasn't for us. We had been used to strolling easily back and forth to the house, taking short walks and enjoying the beautiful scenery that surrounded us. After a few short months and high interest rates, we took the first offer that came our way, and back to the river we went, glad that it was all over. Funny how you can wish for something and think that it's the best thing for you. Then, when you get it, you discover it's not what you wanted at all. With the exception of the expensive move, we'd had to go "there" to get back "here."

I'd never paid a lot of attention to our home once it was built. Made of redwood, this 1680s historic-style structure was very plain-looking, with a steep cedar shake roof. Its look was exactly what we'd intended beside the road overlooking the river. We'd chosen colors that we liked and placed rugs that I had bought years earlier, along with well-worn furniture that had come from both sides of our families. We'd then purchased a few pieces that blended with our antiques, some good and some not so good. But once everything was in place, it wasn't moved again, not even if it had sat in the same spot for thirty years. The store was where I juggled and rearranged merchandise every day, so I was quite happy with the thought of seeing my furniture at home in a familiar setting.

After selling the store, though, I did some extensive housecleaning. I straightened closets, tidied dresser drawers, sorted through old books and found missing objects that I hadn't realized were lost. Carlo did lots of reading, napping and walking his familiar paths along the river. We cooked, ate regular meals and visited our children and grandchildren. I never knew there could be so many hours in a day.

We visited one of the state parks, where I picked up a brochure listing all of the parks in Kentucky. As I scanned it, an idea came to me. Years earlier, we had visited Old Talbott Tavern in Bardstown, Kentucky, thought to be the oldest Western stagecoach stop in America and licensed under Patrick Henry. Its architecture and its guest list, such a fabulous repository of our nation's history, were captivating. Feeling inspired by a book I had once read, I decided to write a combination travel and cookbook, *Favorite Recipes from a Treasury of Country Inns and Lodges*. It was published in 1988.

Why not promote it in the various parks?

Carlo thought it was a superb idea. It would get us out, meeting new people again, but this time it would be on their terms. I had such a passion for the book which took so long to put together that I knew I could sell it. My years of experience in meeting and dealing with people gave me confidence, and I looked forward to the challenge.

With a sense of purpose in the air, we started on our new venture. I did my homework, setting up appointments. We visited thirty-six parks, many of which we had never seen before, and we could now understand why some of our regular customers had made state parks their weekend destinations. I enjoyed all of them, especially the John James Audubon in Henderson.

Our days and weeks were now filled. We loved the open country traveling and thought it was a wonderful transition from being storekeepers to (literally) a day in the park. We had promoted Kentucky all of these years. Now we were finally getting to see all five regions and the amazing diversity of each one.

I had taught Appalachian culture in the elder hostel program at Sue Bennett College, and when I developed my curriculum, I read about these regions and made a comparative study of each. Now we were there, enjoying their natural beauty. We had never known such freedom. There were times when I missed going into the store, but that soon passed with the planning of another trip. Since Kentucky had been so receptive to my book, why not take it into the surrounding states as well? Of course this meant new adventures that fed our insatiable appetites—at least for now.

Phone call after phone call took us into Tennessee, Ohio, Indiana and Illinois, where we found ambassadors for each state. Due to the distances between the parks, we found many interesting sites to explore and ate different kinds of foods. When the weather grew warm, Cokes and hot cups of coffee provided excuses to stop frequently.

We knew that Indians had once roamed the countrysides of Ohio and Illinois. What we didn't know was the heavy influence of Indian themes carried out so beautifully in architecture and artifact collections, especially in Illinois. Like Kentucky, the parks were isolated in the most unpromising spots, but the scenery attracted visitors, giving way to unusual rock formations, wildflowers and trees natural to the areas. The parks were warm and inviting, full of easy hospitality that made us want to come back.

This project took several months. When it was all over, we had a different view of everything. We were more content now, but always open to temptation. Our store on the river was still standing, locked and silent.

Back To School

*F*inding something to occupy our time became increasingly difficult. In the old days the village had been alive with excitement. Now it was replaced by more recent attractions along the exits of I-75. We missed the people, the buying and selling, the unpacking of boxes and the displaying of merchandise to capture customers' attention. It had all been such a vital part of our lives.

But the months went swiftly by, and when Jon, our youngest, started school in 1970, I began commuting as a college freshman. I graduated in 1981 with a degree in elementary education. My children presented me with a pair of gold earrings and a plaque which read: "After many long years, six children and five grandchildren, Momma is declared a teacher."

I substituted for a short time before taking a full-time teaching position. When an opening became available at Livingston Elementary, I figured, why not apply the skills I had been certified for? I met with a committee, and the question was asked, "What do you think is most important in helping a child to learn?" I replied, "A good teacher and a blackboard." I got the job. It's a hectic business, being a schoolteacher, but a rewarding one and never dull.

Schooling and education have always been precious to me. When Carcille, our oldest, began attending first grade, I accompanied her to that handsome red brick building with grades 1-12, its halls and stairways filled with laughing children. I couldn't help recalling the school that I had attended as a small child and how I still loved the memory of it. I wished that my children could have the same delightful experiences I'd had, slipping through the hemlock trees, down the steep hillside of Stone Coal Hollow. There was a small branch that I crossed before coming to the main outside road with its rocky landscape of green maple, oak and birch trees.

There were no houses and no traffic. I had the whole world to myself. I picked wildflowers along the way, found terrapins and snakes and chased rabbits and butterflies. I skipped barefoot along that lonely, dusty road. I soon rounded the last curve that led to the typical one-room country school of the 1930s.

The weathered clapboard structure sat perched on stacked rocks like an old graying bird on her nest, overlooking Little Goose Creek. The building, constructed around 1894, had three twelve-foot windows on each side, and the front door was shaded by a very large tree. And standing in this doorway was Miss Bertha Garrison, ringing her hand bell with a big smile on her face. It was 8:00, time for books.

I quickly jumped into a swaying line that stretched out over the bank and into the dirt road. We marched inside and paused just long enough to set down our dinner buckets. We found our seats. The roll call was often answered with a Bible verse. After the Bible was read by our teacher, we all stood and recited the Pledge of Allegiance to the Flag.

One teacher taught all eight grades, so she began the day with the first grade. We sat on Peabody seats according to grade level and listened as she kept the classes flowing. The older students often helped the slower ones to catch up. It was very important for each child to learn how to read, write and spell correctly. Some of the children learned to form fancy letters at an early age. We carefully guarded our penny pencils and five-cent tablets, because in those days such things were hard to come by, so we wasted nothing. But most of our work was done individually at the blackboard.

The school year was shorter than what we have today. Families needed help in tending their crops. We were eager to go to school, because it was more fun than staying at home and working. Summer days were very hot, and the winter was freezing, with a large potbellied stove that sat in the middle of the room. Even though there was a roaring fire on cold days, the heat could not spread evenly. Children who sat too close were too hot, and those who sat near the windows were too cold. So sometimes we changed seats. There were large cracks in the floor that didn't help either. One student was given the job of starting the fire each morning; he was paid five cents a day. And of course he arrived earlier than the rest of us, giving the fire time to build.

There was a nearby spring which furnished our drinking water, and a filled bucket sat on a stool near the teacher's desk. We all drank from the same dipper and to my knowledge suffered no ill effects. Some of the children brought their own collapsible aluminum cups, which proved to be their undoing. The temptation was too great not to collapse them, spilling water on the floor. To be excused, we simply placed a book on the floor inside the door.

A large, brown, short-haired dog which belonged to one of the Sizemore children came to school every day. When the teacher gave instructions, she simply moved around him as he sprawled right in the middle of the room. There were bullies and pranksters, but it was unheard of to defy or talk back to the teacher. However, we did on occasion stand at the blackboard with our noses in a ring, or sit on the dunce stool or receive a little paddling. That was the last thing anyone wanted, because that meant another one at home for having misbehaved at school.

We all carried our dinners to school in syrup buckets—except for the Garrison children, who packed theirs in colorful lunch pails which their Aunt Lila had bought in Cincinnati and mailed home. Each bucket contained similar foods: fried chicken, ham and fried apples on biscuits. In season we had corn-on-the-cob and ripe, red tomatoes. In every bucket was also a pint jar of room-temperature milk. Apples and pears were an added treat.

The creek bank, hillside and the edge of the road were our favorite places to eat. Some of the older boys sat on a huge rock that looked like it might topple at any moment. We smaller children sat on the foot log that stretched across the creek and dangled our bare feet into the cool running water. After we'd finished eating, we skipped rocks across the stream and looked for tadpoles and minnows. Little Goose Creek, with its clear, sparkling water, served as an ice rink on cold, cold winter days, and when the ice was frozen thick enough, the teacher took the children down there and skated along with them. Those were such happy days.

There was no playground, so during recess we played mumbly peg (with real knives), ante over, ring around the roses, leapfrog and softball. Marbles was a great game too. Both boys and girls joined in. It was played out in the middle of the dirt road—with no danger of traffic, because Charlie Garrison owned the only car up that way, and he didn't come home until he left his office at 5:00 p.m.

We were never bored at school. We explored the woods, made hats and belts from leaves and sticks, showed our art talents by tracing designs in the soft earth. Some, depending upon the designers, were very elaborate.

Everyone looked forward to the spelling bee on Friday afternoon. It was a noisy event. We clapped our hands and stamped our feet. To win was an honor and a challenge that we looked forward to. After school I set out for home. There were two routes I could take, the main road or across the creek on a footlog and through the woods. This was a shorter route, and because of the thick growth of trees, I felt cool even on the hottest days. I could also stop and play a while with a family of children and eat the apples that had fallen on the ground. After enjoying my fill, I entered woods that were so dense, it felt like nightfall. The narrow path seemed to go on forever. I walked as lightly as I could, so I could not hear the rustling leaves under my feet. The silence was broken only when an occasional limb fell to the ground. Each time this happened, my heart just went pitter-patter. Afraid to look back, I kept on moving as quietly as possible until there was a break in the woods at the end. It was a wonderful, warm feeling, because I knew I would soon be home.

Like so many other things in our lives, the little one-room school has vanished from the landscape of America forever. And with it went much of our value system and a sense of knowing right from wrong. We've all come a long way from the innocence of the 1930s—but a lot can still be said for that simple school. In addition to learning the three R's, there was a whole world of knowledge found in just getting there.

The school in Livingston that Carcille entered and where I later taught, with its halls and stairways, was grand compared to the more primitive one that I attended as a child. But the warmth and individual training that all of our children received was similar to that of a much smaller place. It eventually carried all six into the world to compete as successful professionals in their chosen fields.

As a beginning teacher, I noted that the street behind the school was lined with houses that had once been home to the young boys and girls who attended. Now grandparents, old and retired, lived there. Even the principal had grown up and gone to school there, and for the most part, generations of the same families. Livingston was a place that didn't attract much attention. When we first saw that warm red brick building forty years earlier, it was the town's centerpiece. What had once been a flourishing railroad center was now quiet with only a grocery store, post office and a restaurant.

But once inside the school, the building came alive with the comings and goings of laughing children. The freshly painted walls and wooden floors, worn from age and time, were polished and shined to a high gloss. There was beauty and promise. With my schedule I visited each room and wondered where my children had once sat. They'd learned, all six of them, in all of the classrooms, and it gave me pleasure and a warm feeling.

Unfortunately, while I was teaching, two tragedies struck our family. First, we lost our son-in-law Freddie, Betsy's husband and the father of their two daughters. Then, in 1992, after 44 years of marriage and while surrounded by his family, Carlo suddenly slipped away, following a short illness. He was so well-known and respected in lower Kentucky that a friend remarked that his funeral was equal to that of a state occasion. All six children acted as pallbearers, carrying him to rest.

After the service, I rode back down U.S. 25 to the village and to the safety of my home which had always protected me from the outside world—and I collapsed.

Finally, after two weeks, I returned to school. Children would stop halfway down the hall, give me a quick hug and then pass on by without saying a word. Through the grace of God, family, friends and help from these little healing arms, I slowly recovered.

During that time, however, I also received one of the highest compliments of my life. For the school's eighth grade graduation exercises, I was asked to deliver the keynote speech. With love and emotion directed toward my beloved students, I gave my best performance.

But when Livingston Elementary closed its doors forever, I went home again.

Manchester and Little Goose

Springtime in Kentucky, when the dogwoods and red buds begin to bloom, is when we think about home and where we grew up. Manchester is small, even by eastern Kentucky standards. The population might be just over fifteen hundred, and it's believed that the town was built upon timber and other natural resources which attracted early settlers. Goose Creek, a picturesque waterway, runs right through the town. It was once a vehicle to the South Fork of the Kentucky River that ran all the way to the Mississippi and down to New Orleans. Later on, Salt Works at Garrard, a short distance away, played an important part in its development. This little county seat literally spills from the Court House Hill down to the town square, which really isn't a square at all, just a broader area of the street. There are local government buildings, stores, churches and a theater.

It's my town, the town in which I grew up in during the 1940s. I have been gone for over fifty years now, but families and friends that I knew and loved are still there. And as I grow older, I seem to be reminded of it more and more often. When the memories keep pelting me, I realize it is time for me to visit Manchester again.

It was a bright, cool morning as I drove from my home on the Rockcastle River across the parkway into Clay County. The drive turned into a breathtaking mountainscape of glistening sunshine, with redbud and dogwood trees in full bloom—simply magnificent in delicate shades of pink and white.

The years seemed to roll away, and I was home—home to where I had spent sixteen of the first nineteen years of my life. For the moment, the memories had the upper hand.

One thing was certain, I was not a newcomer. I could trace my lineage back to Robert Bowling, who came from England to Virginia in

1660 and married Jane Rolfe, granddaughter of Pocahontas. My family on both sides had lived in Clay County since the early 1800s. For them frontier hardships were a normal part of life as they contributed to local affairs, both economically and politically. In fact, my fourth great-grandfather Robert Julius Baker's home was the site of the first court held in Clay County in 1807. In addition to his judicial interests, he was deeply concerned about the education of his own and his neighbors' children. He secured a teacher from London to tutor them.

Later, Mama (Verda Marcum) rode in an open wagon from Little Goose Creek to Berea Foundation in hopes of getting a formal education. From there she attended Sue Bennett Normal School, continuing a culture that her Scottish ancestral mother had laid out for her. By the time I was born, the Great Depression had taken its toll, and the rich history of our lands had somehow shrunken to a distant memory.

I parked my car and looked around at the streets where I had ridden a bicycle, skipped and roller-skated as a young girl. I had played softball on the courthouse lawn. I also swam in Goose Creek, led cheers, dressed for dates—and the lesser elements of style—washed dishes, dusted and did homework. And I thought to myself how fortunate I had been to have grown up in a place where people cared about other people's children and were bold enough to speak up if they saw them getting out of line.

My formal education was pretty informal. Somewhere between my early beginnings at a one-room school and Manchester High School, where we got a drilling in the basics, and where valuable disciplines were instilled, we could make a choice—to study or not.

The teachers there were trying to teach me the importance of math and science, but I clearly preferred the art of interpretive monologues, cheerleading, Glee Club, dancing and plays, with the exception of my love for history and English, to the instruction. In my junior year I did, however, win the Best Citizenship Award.

The town as I had known it seemed to have been swallowed up by banks and government buildings. True, some of the stores were still in their familiar settings. These things were pleasant to think about. On Main Street alone, there had been at least a dozen stores with interesting window displays and equally interesting proprietors behind them. It was great to see Rice Asher's name still inscribed on his window. I could see him moving around the old oak counters, the signs, the Putnam dye cases and spool boxes. Next was Cicero Feltner's store, and upstairs was Dr. Jordan's office. His daughter Jo Jo and I ran up the steps and found a nickel that her grandmother had left on the window sill. We took it and ran across the street to Taylor Baker's grocery store and bought Hershey's kisses, three for a penny. Then we sat down on the curb out front, divided the candy and ate it. To this day, chocolate has never tasted so good.

Marcum's Department Store, Langdon's and Hensley's were on up the street. The smell of leather in Hensley's still stays with me after all these years. A significant change in the policies of the workplace at that time was their hiring of Harrison Potter, a black man, who fitted patrons with shoes.

Across the street was Burn's Place, known as "The Roost," where the events of the day were hashed over by the men, perched on a bench, heads turning, reveling in the simple pleasures of conversation and without that indispensable item that today's society seems unable to live without—the cell phone.

The Town Tavern was the hot spot for young people. By one o'clock on Saturday afternoons, the tavern was already crowded with boys and girls amusing themselves with conversation, Cokes and dancing. It didn't matter that some of them didn't dance, or that some refused to try, but they were there, sitting on books or on the bench situated at the end of the building.

The tavern really came alive when the juke box's peacock lit up. We hit the floor, salted for slickness, and danced the afternoon away. We waltzed and jitterbugged—to be fancy, we dipped and twirled, shimmied with our shoulders and did the camel walk to the music of Tommy Dorsey, Glenn Miller, Benny Goodman, Cab Calloway and Harry James. Popular songs of the day were "Sentimental Journey," "In the Mood," "String of Pearls," "Elmer's Tune" and the Andrews Sisters' "Don't Sit Under the Apple Tree." It was great to be a teenager in Manchester back then. But when 5:00 p.m. arrived, my grandmother had other plans for me.

Different generations enjoyed the hospitality of the place, but at different times. The switchboard for most of the county was upstairs. As I sat there, I could still see Mayme Howard and Bess Hayes supporting their elbows out the open window on hot afternoons.

Everywhere I looked, there were reminders of the past. The Webb Hotel was a derelict, with its peeling white paint and double front porches.

Political speeches and sermons were heard from these porches, and on Saturdays, it was the gathering place for the locals to see who had come to town. A woman milled through the crowd, playing her hand-pumped accordion, and children and teenagers hung off the carved newel posts. Many years later, when the hotel was finally torn down, one post was found at the home of Helen and Matt Keith, in memory of their courting days.

Reluctant to leave, I looked up and spotted the theater. This was a magical place which transported both young and old to another time for the price of twenty-five cents, ten cents for children. We could not wait for the movies, especially if they were shown in Technicolor. Serials kept us spellbound from one week to the next.

Rebecca Little, noted for her pretty clothes and stunning hats, promised instant glamour to anyone who bought a ticket. On Sunday afternoons she wore these hats inside the ticket booth. After she left, I worked there during my senior year of high school. In my pullover sweaters, pleated skirts, white bobby socks and saddle oxfords, I must have been a shocking contrast to the previous ticket-seller's image.

But there was one annual event that attracted everyone—the Circus. This interruption of normal life sent young and old, anyone who could afford the price of a ticket to their own adventure.

To brighten the wait, strange-looking men with tired, baggy eyes began appearing in town. They nailed bold, colorful posters of clowns and elephants to all buildings, fence posts and telephone poles. Some were nailed on top of the previous year's posters.

Finally the big day arrived. Trucks, sagged and squeaky, rolled slowly through the town square, hauling elephants and lions. Men waved and smiled as they passed by.

Times had not changed much since my father was a little boy—nor had the traveling road show. I was told that he and another child walked the distance from their home to the Circus. When they did not return at the appointed time, my grandmother went searching for them and found them both sound asleep near the animal pen. They were exhausted from watering the elephants.

Sometimes as a young girl, I changed my routine of walking home through town and took a shortcut to the top of the hill. It was a dark detour. One night I heard footsteps behind me. I began to walk faster. The footsteps grew quicker and louder. I became frightened. Then a voice broke the silence. It was Joe Walker, a black man. "Does your grandmother know you come up this way?" he inquired. "Somebody'll grab you." On I walked, with Joe right beside me until we got to the light at the corner of the street. He stopped, clapped his hands together and said, "Now git." I ran home. But before I stepped inside my door, I looked back, and there, standing in the shadows of the street lamp, was the old man making sure I was safely home.

Two other buildings not far apart on the hill reminded me of how much I had been given here. One was the Baptist Church. It was a wooden structure painted white, and the pastor was Brother Walters. He baptized me along with others when I was sixteen in the cool waters of Goose Creek on a Sunday afternoon. And that's where I went to Sunday school, sang songs and met my friends. Our teacher was Mrs. Samples, a lovely lady who had such compassion for the lessons she brought us that she often cried, dabbing her eyes with a soft, white lace handkerchief.

The other was a large two-story, brown and box like, with double porches that stretched across the front. The pillars were brick and chiseled sandstone rock. The railing was also of sandstone rock, and that's where I sat and entertained my friends.

In our working-living room, the brick fireplace was the focal point, and from there everything else seemed to evolve into interesting elements, which to some eyes might suggest clutter. To others, an artist's home—which is exactly what it was.

There was a loom with a half-finished rug and a basketful of colorful carpet balls that I had helped tack together as a small child by the light of a coal-oil lamp. I still have the lamp. Two sewing machines—one an old-fashioned treadle. Patterns, materials and lace, comfortable chairs, a piano, stacks of books, and an antique hall mirror that stood by the front door. The ladies checked their petticoats here.

People were always coming and going, and sometimes before breakfast. One morning Lil Rogers, Mama's hairdresser, dropped by. Clearly in a hurry to get to work, she came right out with it: "When did Lucille get her driver's license?" Knowing that I was not old enough to drive, Mama replied that I didn't have a license, and that we didn't even own a car. Lil went on to say that I had been driving after school the day before toward Burning Springs and that gravels were flying. Now, why would someone report two young people, thrilled at the adventure of speeding in an old model car? I never even asked. It was a very touchy subject.

The Porter Drug Store, once the main artery of the town was no longer there. What a pity. In terms of style and décor, this establishment was way ahead of its time, with its marble soda fountain and handsome mirrored back bar. On lazy afternoons, it was a place of quiet reflection for the ladies who came in to smoke cigarettes and sit with their Cokes. The tinkling of sparkling glasses and soft laughter was all the music that was needed. Ice cream was brought and picked up in dry ice at the depot. Only Sealtest, in vanilla, chocolate, strawberry and sometimes hazelnut, was served there. The windows were decorated with slogans advertising Hava-Tampa Cigars, Coca-Cola and Whitman's Candies. Across the front of the building, there was a draped awning that gave it a look of invitation in hot weather.

The pressed tin ceilings were high and hung with paddle fans. Beautiful shelving with sliding glass doors was filled with patent medicines. Most everything from Cardui, Golden Medical Discovery, Lydia & Pinkhams, Hadacol, Miles Nervine to Walko Tablets for baby chicks could be found there. Fine stationery and Parker and Schaffer fountain pens could be purchased, along with Coty creams and powders. I was more interested in the Schaffer pens, along with Emeraude and Evening in Paris perfumes.

This store, operated by Dr. Porter, never failed to generate hospitality and drama, but the jewel of the place was his wife Cleo, a niece of my grandmother. Short and full-figured, she had thick, auburn hair that framed a pretty round face, with a little flirtation of soft ringlets on the left side of her forehead. Cleo was familiar with all of the business. She used Pacquins hand cream, never put a lid on a powder box or rolled lipstick back inside the tube. She smoked Chesterfields and was totally unaffected by the drama she created in her tiny high-heeled shoes. She was a fabulous pianist and gave lessons inside her turn-of-the-century home, where she was born and had lived her entire life. Despite suffering from asthma, Cleo was full of hospitality and was comfortable with any age group from any walk of life.

Porter's was a destination, both social and clinical. And at any time of the year you might see the frontier nurses come riding in for supplies astride their big fat horses—or Mrs. Turner, who offered an added element of refinement to the profession, as she swept along the

Vegetable and herb garden

Koula Verda and Carlo David

Carly Rae and Betsy Lucille, first day of school.

Ellie Jame and Emma Kate

Laura Whitney and John Zackary

Lucille and family at garden dedication at Cumberland College. Dusty, grand-daughter Carly Rae, Betsy, Jon, Carcille, Buzz.

This Garden Is Dedicated To
Lucille and Carlos Carloftis
And Their Family Who Sought
Cumberland College
As A Source of Higher Education

Designed by Jon Carloftis

Dedicated June 28, 2003

The best place to seek God is in a garden.
You can dig for Him there.
                        Bernard Shaw

Lucille Bowling Carloftis.

sidewalks in her crisp white uniform, cap and navy blue cape. At any rate, it would have been difficult not to have had a warm, comforting feeling whenever you saw them. They looked so regal, yet predictable.

Any sudden activity in town brought a flurry of excitement—like the time when a big, black Cadillac drove in and parked right in the middle of the square. It attracted a considerable amount of attention, especially from the men. After a few minutes of looking out Porter's window, one man walked outside to get a better view. He inspected it from all sides, then stooped down and looked up underneath it. Other times a pretty girl might arrive, deeply tanned and wearing white short shorts.

Comic strips like Al Capp's Lil Abner and Dick Tracy were discussed with fun and gusto by some of the professionals who stopped by the soda fountain for a Coke. Whatever it was, they had a spirited self-confidence and a keen sense of humor.

I should add that there was not a lot of coming and going, except for the Black Brothers Buses. A favorite expression in departure was, "I'm going out on the MAIN line."

Manchester offered a guaranteed charm filled with friendliness, character and style. There was no shortage of fine clothing in town and many people dressed beautifully, in suits from Lexington, Cincinnati and Louisville. But for the most part, clothes were hand-sewn from Simplicity, McCalls, Butterick, and Vogue Patterns. These, of course, would be considered designer couture today.

I can still see Josephine and Linda Lou Hensley spinning around on their roller skates in hunter green capes, Jean Baker in soft, elegant linens, and Dr. and Mrs. Anderson, perfectly groomed, who were reminders of a Currier & Ives painting as they gently strolled up and down the sidewalk in the late evening. Both were in their advanced years, and Mrs. Anderson, her complexion still good, told Mama that hers would look even better if she used Revlon's Moon Drops.

Clara Burchell's store had been closed for years, but it was still a place worth remembering. Stalks of bananas hung inside the windows, and other fresh fruit sat nearby. She sold everything from garden seed to old-fashioned horehound candy, and in season, locally grown garden vegetables. Fat hens were practically on foot.

She took great joy in this small establishment that distinguished itself from today's supermarkets with their mass-produced goods, and she kept it open, welcoming customers until she reached a very old age.

On past was the First National Bank, and tucked between the Hardware Store and Hen's Corner, was the Krystal Kitchen. During lunch hours, we crowded the place and ate ten-cent hot dogs and drank five-cent Cokes. The restaurant was about five blocks from school, and if we finished fast enough, we went to Hen's Corner and danced a tune or two, then rushed back to school before the tardy bell rang.

I had often recalled all of this, and had wanted to come back again and just sit alone. Now, somewhat to my own surprise, I'd done it.

There was a distinct rhythm of slow-moving cars as they crisscrossed the square to Richmond Road, Town Branch, East Manchester and to the Courthouse Hill. As in any small town, colorful stories abound, and they are a part of its people and its woven character. The real riches of life, though, are not buildings or things; but smiles, laughter and people sitting on their front porches greeting those who pass by.

Richness is also about fragrant gardenias worn in lapels, men tipping their hats to ladies, being affectionately called "Happy" by Mr. Howard, and Mrs. Potter's beaten biscuits. Those are the things we remember. Yes, it was good to go back home.

Time In Lexington

Lexington, in the center of the bluegrass region, is a world-class horse town surrounded by miles of white fences and unparalleled farmland. It's also a fashionable area, with high-profile residents and a home called Ashland, the Henry Clay estate.

After graduating from the University of Kentucky in 1987, Jon had gone to New York City, founded his own rooftop garden design business and built it up. But he dreamed of opening his own store in Lexington.

Finding the right space was not without its problems. We wanted a courtyard to showcase fountains, specialty plants and other gardening treasures so popular with the horticultural set. Eager to get started, we found a location on the corner of Woodland and Maxwell Streets. It was in the old part of town—but there was no courtyard or parking, except along the street.

Jon asked me if I would like to manage it. At first I thought it was a ridiculous notion, but with pleasant memories of our past businesses, I accepted the challenge and looked forward to the change. Jon brought pot after pot of flourishing green plants inside, told me the name of each, and then gave me a review quiz.

I failed it.

"Momma," he said, "these ladies here in Lexington are real gardeners. Please don't call everything 'bushes.'"

My whole world had been the national forest with only the wildflowers that grew in the woods along the river bank. So I admitted I wasn't a gardener and carried my expertise into the field of merchandising. Jon came to my rescue, joking to his customers that the extent of my gardening experience was caring for his grandmother's gardenia plant, now more than forty years old. He went on to say that anyone who could grow a gardenia in a washtub and keep it healthy and thriving for over four decades had to know something about plants. It made a great story.

We were welcomed warmly by the community and achieved a kind of sophisticated aura, carrying both gardening supplies and fine gifts. There was always a pot of fresh flowers near the front door to greet our customers. We were photographed and written about in local magazines which described our style and the quality of merchandise that we offered. It was fun meeting new people and attending their social events. But building a business is never easy. Most of our walk-in buyers were in a hurry and very short of time. And when cold weather set in, people strode briskly up and down the streets, barely stopping long enough to glance at our window displays. At the Indian village, people stopped on their way in to pet the family dog or gently stroll around the grounds, looking at the chickens and peacocks. Then they would pause and warm themselves at our potbellied wood burning stove before starting to shop. Things were less hectic back then and much more inviting.

Still, in Lexington we made friends. Early one morning the freight men came to make a delivery. It was a sofa, custom-made and of fine design. With its heavy packing, it was too large to get inside our door. I watched the men turn it up, over and around. Then they set it down and declared it was impossible to maneuver inside. I sent it back.

The next day, I called to see if it had left the depot, and if not, I had a plan. Jon's friend would bring his pickup truck, park it outside and take the sofa home with him for storage. A few hours later, I walked across the street to check on the sofa and became suspicious when I saw children's car seats inside the truck. Then I spotted another truck in the same color, make and model, on the corner side of the street. Oh, no. I panicked.

My rescuers were fireman who carried the sofa to the right truck. I thanked them. Could I do anything for them in return? They shook their heads with a smile. But a great mistake had been averted, and by the end of that week, the entire fire department was enjoying a fine, home-baked Hershey Bar chocolate cake that Carcille had made.

The bicycle shop across the street reminded me of a place back in Pineville. One summer afternoon my friend and I passed by the sport mart, stopped and admired their window display. She told me that when she and her husband first married, he'd handed her his paycheck. She went in and bought a new Red Flyer bicycle. It never crossed her mind that the money was for paying bills. But, she said, he was a reasonable man.

So every weekday for four years and two months, I traveled an hour each way up and down I-75. I drove through snowstorms and heavy rainfalls. I saw magnificent rainbows. I also saw wrecks, cows grazing on the wrong side of the fence, a blonde woman wearing hot pink shorts and riding a tricycle. I even saw history being made with the construction of the high bridge at Clays Ferry. There was always a comfortable rhythm as I carefully observed the speed limit and watched the other cars and trucks sway and swerve down the highway.

Each morning I allowed myself a brief but dramatic stopover for coffee and breakfast somewhere between Livingston and Lexington. I found several good places to eat, and since breakfast has always been my favorite meal, it gave me a good start for my day. One morning I stopped at a local restaurant and ordered half-and-half coffee. The young girl behind the counter, trying to be agreeable, handed me my cup and said, "I put the decaf on top."

Each night, when I left the lights of the city, I drove a steady pace back to the country. The return trip seemed easier. In winter, due to short days and early nightfalls, I thought the houses I passed looked all wrapped up in coziness as lamps shone through their windows. In summer, the long evenings were dressed in glorious sunsets. I often pulled off the highway to admire the majesty of it all.

Post Office built by my great-uncle, Morgan Bowling in 1916 and moved from McWhorter.

Home Again

The store at the village had been closed for more than four years. The parking lot was potholed and rough. The roof was leaky. The interior was difficult to heat and cool. The family talked it over, and what came as a real surprise was the unanimous decision to simply tear it down. At Jon's Lexington store, there had been no room for a courtyard to display his fountains and pots. He was ready to build.

We had a plan.

We made a detailed drawing of a new store, using the same foundation as the old one, except that we made it much smaller. We would build an early Colonial clapboard that would be more in keeping with our home's style, and we would paint it red. We were excited. A local craftsman would be our construction manager.

There was also the possibility of restoring another rundown building on the property. The blacksmith shop would be moved and with cedar fencing would become the focal point for a vegetable and herb garden. The schoolhouse was moved to accommodate overnight guests. It was self-contained, with a screened-in porch overlooking the river. The potting shed was an interesting addition, and it was showcased at the Atlanta Flower Show, filled with tools and pots. It now sits near the store and has its own bricked-in courtyard, complete with benches. It's where I often sit and have my morning coffee.

Work almost stopped, however, when the carriage house was built. It was, I thought, in the wrong location. But now that it's here, I realize it's exactly right. Bridges again connect the property.

In the early spring of 2000, we opened our doors to tourists. It was a breathless moment for me to walk across the foot bridge from my house and begin greeting customers once more. We all knew it would take time to build our clientele, but I was used to that, and I kept myself busy with writing, rearranging merchandise and sitting outside in the courtyard beside the store.

Gone were the covered wagons, the teepees and other Native American memorabilia that had defined our early business years. The forts were no longer there either, and I regretted that, because they'd been built from logs that dated back to the late 1700s. The landscape remained the same, however—quiet and peaceful, except for the cars passing and the train across the river. We loved to hear it blow its whistle as it rounded the bend at Hazel Patch. Carlo always had a special fascination with trains. He had a collection of train whistles, one of which was on display in our store.

So much had changed since the time when we opened our first business back in 1955. The salesmen used to drive out to see us, bringing their merchandise from which to select. After we'd closed the store at dusk, they would carry in bags and bags filled with items, spread them out across the floor, and we would often keep buying things far into the night. We formed close relationships with those companies. They soon learned that we would never carry anything offensive or off-color, not even so much as a postcard. We bought from several different vendors, and lots of people came to sell their wares. One salesman told us a tale of trying to establish a new account, and when the store owner informed him that he wasn't interested in purchasing anything new, the salesman replied, "Well, just let me show you what I have. I haven't seen it myself in quite a while."

Later came the travel trailers. Everything would already be laid out, attractively displayed, and we would walk inside to look it over, then place our order. Shortly thereafter, the salesmen would pull out and head eagerly toward their next appointments.

Now it's all about gift shows in Knoxville and Atlanta—floors and floors of beautiful displays. For the most part, the warm, personal touch is absent. No more sharing of homemade canned goods to take back to families. No more bringing each other up to date with stories about our children. Everyone is in too much of a hurry. Long ago, one of our salesmen would bring his wife along, stay a couple of days at a nearby motel, take our inventory and then visit with us for hours. Such rich experiences. I truly missed the good old days of merchandising—but I always knew I could still do my part to bring them back.

Open and airy, with glossy wood floors and large windows for spacious outside views, the store now has the look of the garden house it was always meant for. Today, the Rockcastle River Trading Company is a stylish, upscale home and garden store, decorated with elegant pots, fine linens, handmade cherry furniture, bistro tables and chairs from France, dinnerware from Italy, lamps, garden accessories and exotic soaps, scented candles and lotions.

At one end of the store sits the wooden counter from our original establishment. It is over a hundred years old. The huge mirror that rests behind it is flanked by two ornamental lamps from the Continental Hotel in Pineville, built in 1913. Photographs of some of the Indians who were here in our early days hang proudly nearby.

With Jon's effort and growing notoriety, we soon began attracting garden clubs and travel writers. All of the buildings on our property are now painted in our signature color, red. We have, once again, become a destination.

On September 14, 2002, I received this letter from George Percy, senior vice-president of Geiger and Associates Public Relations:

Dear Mrs. Carloftis,

Thank you again for your generous hospitality in welcoming the writers on our August and September press trips to eastern Kentucky, which our firm conducted on behalf of the Southern and Eastern Kentucky Tourism Development Association. Both groups of writers appreciated your wonderfully unique store, easily the best in eastern Kentucky (and maybe the whole state), your magnificent house and gardens, and your own considerable warmth and charm. The refreshments in your house were an extra treat.

And to show our appreciation, with food and entertainment to promote our business, we have annual spring and fall Open Houses. For these events our family comes together to preside over them, thereby creating a renewal of interest in our area and a business which has spanned fifty years of struggle and triumph. We also host garden clubs, and we always invite our guests to walk around our grounds and enjoy the natural setting, the forest, the river, the peace and solitude that we have never for a moment allowed ourselves to take for granted.

Shortly after one of these events, I received a note from a visitor and her daughter:

I want to thank you for holding onto your and your husband's dream until we could share in it too. It was like rediscovering a bit of our own past.

Visiting Friends – And
A Time To Remember

*I*t was twilight when we arrived at the Goddard house in the fall of 2004. The evening was unusually warm for late October, and we were looking forward to this visit. It was perfect weather. We saw people outside raking leaves and walking their dogs.

We parked out front and just stared at the handsome two-story log house. It was the time of day when everything takes on a kind of blue hue. All lit up, it looked like a jewel box framed in majestic Burr oak trees, three hundred years old and with limbs as thick as normal tree trunks.

Monnie and her friend Randy were sitting on the front porch. Standing in the doorway was an elegant gentleman wearing a white jacket, ready to serve us refreshments.

We stepped inside the rooms, vivid and colorful with art and family photographs. Everything was interesting, and there was no shortage of genuine Southern hospitality. At the table everyone enjoyed a delicious dinner of pork, fresh vegetables and a specialty dish of fried green tomatoes, cooked to perfection by the hostess herself, and right before our very eyes. I reveled in conversation that was filled with stories of our earliest and most memorable times in the kitchen and at the dining table. The evening was off to a good start.

We took a stroll through a natural alley that had once been a railroad bed and walked by an old cemetery with headstones dating back to the 1700s. We saw prize chickens and a rooster from the same bloodlines as the fowls that Monnie's grandparents had raised.

But what intrigued me most were the giant trees and the care that Monnie was giving them. Three thousand gallons of water were poured annually to wet their roots, and they were carefully pruned, keeping them windproof. As we stood and admired them, one could almost hear the hoofs of the buffalo as they thundered past. A low-settling fog added to the atmospheric grandeur.

Developers would not show their faces here. Monnie would see to that. She loved the land and was preserving the wealth of it for future generations . I felt a kind of kinship for her appreciation of place, just as I do here on the river. It was hard to leave, but it was time to go, and as we drove away, I was reminded of the first log house I had ever visited more than sixty years earlier. I rode there on horseback.

The Philpot house sat near the dirt road that led to Kincaid. It was pre-nineteenth century, built of hand- hewn logs and chinked with yellow clay mud. The architectural style of two stories had huge rock chimneys on each end and a dog trot with picturesque views of running water out back. The countryside was so rough and rugged that only horses and mule-drawn wagons passed by.

The furnishings were primitive, yet handsome. The centerpieces of the rooms were the beds. They were voluptuous, with feather-filled ticking covered in white muslin, embroidered in intricate designs and pulled tightly over the tops. I can still see one of those coverlets, stitched with a large basket filled with delicate, colorful flowers in all shapes and sizes.

Lucy Philpot loved flowers. Her yard was hard packed and swept clean with a broom. There was not a loose blade of grass to be seen. Flower beds were encircled with creek rocks, and they looked like works of art, which is exactly what they were. Even as a child, I was in awe of Lucy's gardening skills and her use of harmoniously blended colors. Looking back now, I marvel at the toil and sacrifice of time that she put into that garden to make her part of the world a more beautiful place.

The Philpots were farmers. When spring arrived Lucy was ready to work outdoors with her hands in the soil, planting vegetables and flower seeds. I had grown up in the country until I was twelve years old, so I felt the same connection to the land and to this kind of life.

In those days, the tradition was to help others to "lay-by" their crops. It was called a "working," a celebration that symbolized the beauty and dignity of hard work and gathering. As it turned out, I was there the day the neighbors came to lend a helping hand. They brought their wives along to do the cooking and to socialize with one another. All day they prepared food, and by the time the men came in from the fields, dinner was placed on tables that had been set up in the yard.

What a feast for the eyes! Fried chicken, chicken and dumplings, large platters of ham and redeye gravy, beef and pork and an array of fresh garden vegetables, all topped off with luscious desserts. I amused myself by walking around the tables, looking at everything. I stayed as near to the chocolate pies as I could.

Thanks to my close family connections to the Philpots and the Benges, I was able to enjoy many late summer visits to Kincaid. I would not have missed those days, and I wish that they were still here.

But that's not all that was happening in this wonderful countryside. Feuds that had started in the early 1930s still lingered in pockets of Appalachia—and it was no different here. Riding his horse home one night, Bill Philpot, called Black Bill, husband of Lucy and father of their five grown sons, was ambushed, killed and left by the roadside. It was a dark and sad day in Kincaid.

Ella Benge cooked and worked at my grandmother's farm. Grandma, my daddy's mother, was also the postmaster. During the Great Depression years, work was scarce, and Ella had a small child to raise. So they made their home with my grandmother until Agnes grew up. My father, Robert Franklin Bowling, worked in the timber business, so he was gone a lot. I remember he was a handsome man who wore corduroy pants, plaid flannel shirts and lace-up work shoes. I once heard him say he'd rather have a pocketful of shiny little rocks than to have a pocketful of money that he wouldn't spend. Mama, soft-spoken, petite and pretty, was unable to care for me, so I lived with Grandma too. If it had to be, the situation was ideal. Agnes played and took care of me, and I loved her dearly.

When she started dating, I was made to feel very much a part of her courtship. One of the Philpot boys had caught her eye, and on Sunday afternoons, when he came calling, she dressed me up in my pongee dress, white silk stockings, white lace-up shoes, and tied a pretty ribbon in my hair. Then she set me down on my grandmother's tufted brown leather fainting sofa and told me not to move until Lawrence got there.

To this day, I can still see him as he came riding fast on horseback, his necktie blowing in the wind. They eventually married, and when their first baby was born, they named her Lucille, after me.

Ella's two brothers, Tom and Henry, lived in Kincaid too, and with Agnes staying at the Philpots, the trips to visit there became more frequent. I was sometimes invited to tag along, and since the arrival of the new baby, I couldn't wait to go.

Tom and Henry's house was a small board and batten, roughhewn and extremely immaculate. They tended a garden, had their own cow for fresh milk and raised chickens. And they were both known for doing all kinds of farm work. Ella stayed in the kitchen for the most part while we were there, cooking and preparing good, wholesome food, while I played the Victrola. I stood on a chair and watched the spinning record go around for hours, climbing off the chair and winding it up whenever it ran down. My favorite song was, "I want the waiter for my daughter, I want the waiter with the water for my daughter." When I wasn't listening to music, the cover was closed and the oil lamp set upon it.

One night just after dark, rocks were hurled against the side of the building. They came with such force that the small house shook. I trembled and cried.

One of the men grabbed the lamp off the Victrola and blew it out. Then he whispered, "Crawl under the beds." We all did, and after a while, the rocks stopped coming. Then there was silence.

A Marvelous Journey

*B*etween my twin roles as a mother and a storekeeper, there was never much time left for luncheons or visits with friends and neighbors. So I dedicated myself to my family and my work. The store has always been and remains for the most part my social life. I greet visitors from across the country and from foreign lands. I make it fun. I wear my wide-brimmed hat, and sometimes I serve tea and cookies. I always toast someone's birthday or anniversary, if it's mentioned, with a reading, or to change the flavor, I recite a poem. It's been a marvelous adventure, and I've led a rich, full life without ever leaving the banks of the Rockcastle River.

I've also been active on important boards that serve our community, all the while thinking I was doing my proper share as a concerned citizen. One summer the Health Planning Council sent Mildred Winkler and me as delegates to a seminar in Dallas, Texas. Mildred was a nurse and a close friend from my Pineville days. I had already performed my duties on that board as best I could, but this trip widened my knowledge considerably on the subject of health care.

Truthfully, I have never been very organized, and I know that has brought stress and agony to members of my family. Being a romantic, I've always believed that it made everyday events a little more interesting. Except for a couple of times.

I believe that everyone should serve on a jury at least once. I did. But one morning during the trial I overslept. The sheriffs came after me and insisted that I had better get to the Courthouse immediately. Unable to find my own shoes, I slipped my feet into Betsy's high-heeled platform sandals.

When I arrived, the courtroom was stone silent. As my footsteps tapped down the aisle, I had the distinct feeling that everyone was staring at me. All I could think of was the old story of the billy goats clattering on the rickety bridge.

Holding my breath, I took my seat up front. The Judge, granite-faced, ordered me to stand. Then he addressed me sternly and said I was to never enter his courtroom late again.

Later that afternoon I was delivering brochures to the Berea rest area and told the attendant what had occurred. Startled, he informed me that I could have been arrested and sent to jail. And to further emphasize the seriousness of it all, he said he knew a man in Richmond who had actually spent several hours locked up for the very same offense. My mind could hardly take the picture.

I had learned one thing. I never wanted to serve on a jury again.

A year or so later I received a notice summoning me to the Post Office to pick up a registered letter. My knees nearly buckled. I laid the postcard aside and told myself, I've already paid my dues to the court system.

After five days I received another card. That's when I finally decided to drive down the river to the Livingston Post Office. When I walked inside to the first window, there it was—a long white business envelope from a law office in Tallahassee, Florida. I could not imagine what this was all about.

Then I opened it—and nearly fainted. With gratitude, saying nothing, I headed for home.

I had been named an heir to—the Sheldon Tibbott estate in Cleveland, Ohio. In addition, an interest in a Choy Lee sailboat, moored along side the coastal waters of Shell Point near Crawfordsville, Florida.

We sold it.

Another run-in with the law occurred just recently.

With all of the elements of a melodrama, Carcille and I had scheduled a last-minute departure from home to an event with the Bluegrass Conservancy. Arriving late at the Gainesborough Horse Farm, we drove up to the gate. It opened and closed behind us. We drove past one barn and then past another. The landscape was simply breathtaking at every turn. We could hardly believe that we were there. But we drove around and around and could not find the main house. By now we were giving up the whole idea of attending the event and turned around to leave, but we could not get out of the gate.

There was the usual dramatic blackout. We were in the dark in every sense of the word. Then a patrol car with flashing lights met us. As a rule, my teeth chatter whenever I see lights flashing. A portly officer in full uniform wasted no time demanding to know, with an icy stare, how we'd gained entrance in the first place.

We told him that we were supposed to attend a party. "There's no party here," he replied. We insisted that we had an invitation—or rather it would be waiting for us at the door. Again he said, "Nothing is going on here."

He escorted us outside the gate. But before letting us go, he checked with the farm's main office. We overheard the patrolman's demand to the gentleman at the screen to know why he had let us in. It seemed that we had the same make and model car of whomever lived there. The officer said, "Their car is navy blue," to which the gentleman replied, "It looks black on the screen." Finally, after several calls, it was established that the event was scheduled at the Calumet Horse Farm. We had been given the wrong name.

By now we were the only ones who seemed calm and unruffled.

Off They Go To College

For many years I wondered if I had robbed my children of a normal home and a stable upbringing. All of that traveling and chasing around! That steady stream of colorful characters coming and going. Those hundreds of opportunities for getting into mischief. Perhaps Carlo and I would have done better to have given them a well-established family by having settled in Pineville.

Finally, to soothe my conscience, I asked the children, now grown, to tell me their fondest childhood memories. I received nearly the same answer from all of them—they'd loved being together, playing in the woods, swinging over the river on grapevines, the wild life, watching the sunsets and the storm clouds roll in, building play houses out of cardboard boxes, running through the cane thickets, the mock gunfights and learning firsthand the Indian culture and how they created their beadwork, pottery and baskets.

All summed up, it seemed to be the natural and native entertainment that they enjoyed most. When they went away to college, each one asserted his or her individuality. I liked entering their world and watching things take shape through their eyes. After a while we came to realize that their young days here were only a part of their lives, that they had all grown up and had become admirable, self-reliant people.

So, here I am, still on the river, and they're out chasing their own dreams. When I think about them, not the least of their accomplishments as college graduates and professionals, are their abilities to get things done through hard work and without wasting too much time. I've always valued their commitments to their goals and shared them with salesmen, friends and to whomever else would listen to their latest achievements. Living on the grounds next to our business, we were unable to separate our family life from our work, which revolved around the whole affair.

Let me tell you, at a certain point in our lives we had four teenagers at once. And like most parents, we had a few "uprisings" from time to time. But they never amounted to anything more than what we could handle either at home or at school. Our children all knew that their teachers had our full backing and support. Perhaps they were afraid to create any real mischief! At any rate, I'm very grateful.

I was determined to refrain from too many personal stories, but there we were, inexorably woven and bound together by our remote location. I find it noteworthy, then, to offer a glimpse into each of the children's adult lives, exciting and adventurous, because they are all working with people. But more than that, they're all earning reputation and status by helping their fellow man.

It was Carcille, solid and dependable, who set the pace for the rest of the family. When the time came for her to go away to college, Laura Durham, the school librarian, asked if we had ever thought about Cumberland College in Williamsburg in the foothills of the Cumberland Mountains, its streets lined with graceful old homes and beautiful flower gardens. Its curriculum clearly attracts not only mountain students, but others from across the country as well. I had heard about it from a graduate who recalled that local families often invited students into their homes for afternoon tea. This was definitely the place for our Carcille, not too large or impersonal. But alas, we had waited too long. Registration was closed, and all of the beds were filled.

With one phone call after another to President Boswell, I explained that it would be no hardship for Carcille to share a room with two other girls. She came from a large family, and if necessary, we would furnish a cot for her to sleep on. Dr. Boswell replied, "Bring her on." In her haste and excitement before leaving, however, Carcille stepped on a needle and broke it off inside her foot. That delayed her a little, but not much. In time, in fact, she established a Cumberland tradition, with several other members of the family attending, including myself and three grandchildren.

She had grown up and was the first of our children to marry and leave home. Her courtship was carried out at the college, and she married fellow student Clyde Burchette. They have two children, Laura Whitney and John Zachary. Carcille had a tremendous presence of mind, even as a small child. Once she had discovered the structure of mathematics, she pursued her interests and eventually became head of the math department where she had taught for many years. She was declared by some to have been one of the best math teachers in the state for having prepared students for institutions of higher learning. She now coordinates her district's gifted and talented program. Active in both school and community affairs, she's a gracious hostess and interested in just about everything.

Buzz always loved music. The plan was for him to attend Cumberland College as a music major. For three years he had traveled two weeks each summer with the USA School Band, playing flute in Japan, London, Ireland, Scotland, Canada and several cities throughout the United States. But music was not to be his vocation. Instead politics caught his eye, along with the governing aspects of the people. We wondered aloud if he had made the right decision, but through diligence and progress he is now in his fourth term as County Judge Executive, a first ever in our county. An avid reader, he simply loves the adventure of walking the dogs, hiking, exploring and white water rafting.

When it came time for Koula to go to college, she chose a career in cosmetology, married Darrell Collinsworth and had one child, Koula Verda. After a few years they permanently went their separate ways. Although Koula held a degree in elementary education, she never taught school. Instead her flair as a hairstylist led her into owning her own salon. But what really set her apart was her soft voice and her warm gentle manner which captivated the hearts of people who knew her. She later married David Shivel, and they had one son, Carlo David.

The acknowledged sportsman in the family is Dusty. A hunter, avid fisherman and storyteller, he likes nothing better than to get into his Chevrolet pickup truck and listen to his beloved '70s and '80s music or board his high-powered bass boat and go to the lake on weekends. Competitive in spirit, he teaches health and physical education--and is a highly respected football coach, not to mention a devoted husband to his wife Toni and father to their two little girls, Emma Kate and Ellie Jane.

Betsy represents her school district's homebound program, created for children unable to attend regular classes. Her free spirit and colorful sense of drama give her the ability not only to teach, but to get along with her students' families as well. She brings them happiness and fun. Like her parents, Betsy is an adventurer and loves to travel. She married Freddie Overbey, and their two children are Carly Rae and Betsy Lucille.

Jon had a much different vision. He always loved working with his hands and could turn the most common elements into something lovely. After graduating from University of Kentucky, he moved to New York City and hit the rooftops with his own special brand of gardening expertise. Now a nationally renowned garden designer and lecturer, his work has been featured in many magazines and on television. He also built a garden at the University of the Cumberlands (formerly Cumberland College) dedicated in honor of our family. An overflow crowd of people attended, simply brimming with excitement, and cheering him on in their pretty summer outfits and flowered hats. Jon's book, *First A Garden,* was released in the spring of 2005. He now has a second book, *Beyond the Windowsill,* a beautiful edition and very informative.

Traveling with Jon is like being in the eye of a storm. He's exhausting, stimulating and can't resist the temptation of good food or visiting beautiful gardens. He might show up dressed in an Armani suit or work boots and outlandish–looking straw hat. His client list includes the rich and famous of New York City. And I've enjoyed luncheons with some of them when he was honored with others from across the country for artistic achievement at the Museum of the City of New York. I was escorted to the front row. Each designer was recognized with four giant slides. One of Jon's slides showcased our place here on the river. Afterward one lady approached me and said, "Now I know where Jon comes from."

When Jon's first book was published, the youngest son of Malcolm Forbes hosted a book opening party for friends and clients at their Museum on Fifth Avenue. Our family attended this star-studded event. One of the amenities was a museum tour. Miniature sailboats and other interesting memorabilia, including a collection of tiny vases of flowers made of gold and precious gems, were on display. Christopher Forbes later pointed toward the buffet table and said to Buzz, "I know where that came from." Buzz replied, "Yes, that is a Kentucky Country Ham."

One of Jon's clients was so enamored of her garden that she gave him several tickets to opening night at the Chelsea Flower Show. Carcille, Betsy and I were among the lucky ones to attend. It was spring—but the cold rain did not keep Prince Charles, Camilla or Queen Elizabeth away. Nor did it dampen our sense of adventure as we strolled amidst beautiful flowers and witnessed British hospitality at every turn. We missed seeing the royals, but embraced a special affection for the gardens. And although having no distinct taste for duck, I can only say it was surprisingly delicious.

We had seen a whole world beyond our native state and the Rockcastle River.

But the saddest day in all of our lives was when we lost Koula at age 45 to breast cancer. There are no words adequate enough to express the grief and sorrow of losing one's child. It's a time when the soul, in order to go on living, must simply become calm and quiet and surrender itself to God. I believe in prayer and in unseen angels. I have found it to be true that through faith and prayer you can draw the strength and courage for anything that comes your way.

By today's standards our children led a very simple life. There were no TVs, telephones, computers or video games. The patio in front of our house was a noisy place, where they hopped and skipped, twirled and danced, practiced cheers for basketball games—fascinated all the while by their bright reflections in the windows. This was their whole world. It was those everyday amusements and being close to nature which enhanced their spirit of exploration and adventure. I now have eight grandchildren to enjoy. And they have grown up in a much different society than their parents did.

Blessings And Reflections

What has prompted me to write this story? Nostalgia? Some inner force? A need to commemorate a small slice of Kentucky history? Perhaps it was the young woman who came to my door one day not long after we'd closed the store. When I told her we were no longer in business, she literally became distraught. "But this place is my heritage!" she cried.

Maybe it was another woman who rang my doorbell, and when I invited her inside, she declined, saying, "I didn't come to visit. I just stopped by to see how you are." Then she slipped out of sight.

Perhaps it was the memory of LaRue Paytiamo, who inspired me in so many ways.

One morning when I walked across the bridge to the store, I spotted a cardboard box sitting on the hood of my car. I walked over to take a closer look. It was filled with fresh garden vegetables. I unpacked them and found stacked in the bottom several old magazines, dating back to 1917: *Ladies Home Journal, Home Comfort* and *Today's Housewife.*

We ate the vegetables. We read the magazines, some of which I still keep. I never knew where they came from until months later. The Brooks family from Wady, Kentucky, stopped by to tell me they had left them...as they were passing through.

It's summertime, 2005, already. The insects are humming, the birds are singing, and the sun is extremely hot. The landscape is still green, although we've had a very dry season. It has kept me busy with watering the pots. The flowers have been strikingly beautiful, cascading over and into the different shapes and sizes of their containers.

Like all other seasons in my life, even though some have been clouded by tragedy, I have tried to make a contribution to the common good of all those who enter my door—if by nothing more than a smile and a warm welcome.

The vegetable garden promised to be a good one this year, and it was. Lettuce with green onions, lightly tossed with hot bacon fat, an old Southern dish, is a favorite of mine, and I have enjoyed it often. Now red chili peppers are growing in its place.

Visitors admired our purple cabbage, scarlet beans, garlic bulbs, holly hocks, tomatoes and a variety of kitchen herbs we shared with friends. The garden is small, but showy—the cedar fencing intertwined with old-fashioned climbing roses and bordered with bright yellow mums and black-eyed susans.

I've been so busy this year that I hardly realized when spring fell softly into summer. There are so many different kinds of birds now, but a little wren has taken up residence in one of my window boxes. The pansies will have to share their space.

Lots of cleaning and the building of rock steps has gone on—and an aviary has just been completed, adding color and balance to the property. It's home to a beautiful blue-necked peacock and two ring-necked pheasants.

Everywhere I look, I see adventures and memories, intertwining the old with the new. Indian baskets, pottery, stone-carved peace pipes and other artifacts line the shelves of bookcases flanked on each side by totem poles, made here at the village by William Lossiah, one of our original cast members. Other memorabilia from those early days are evident in my home, and there's a story for each piece.

My reflections are interrupted by the beating hooves of the miniature horses that come inside the corral to drink water and to get their daily ration of sweet feed. Their pasture, wooded and green, was once the setting for the Indian village and frontier town. Now the only remnants left are the schoolhouse, the post office and the livery stable which shelters the horses.

I walk inside the blacksmith shop, and there sits the old, one-seater buggy, still shining, that I kept in the store so long ago to display whatever was of the moment. The potbellied stove beside the door is still a reminder that on cold, windy days there's nothing better to warm up to than coal or wooded heat. We bought the stove off the side of the road and paid $10 for it. When Buzz saw it later in a Sears & Roebuck reproduction catalogue, he joked, "You got cheated. That stove costs only $8.88."

That first summer, Jon and Dusty spent most of their time in our riverboat town, full of the noise of gunfights, surrey rides, cruises on a paddle-wheeler and stage shows. Before long they knew every part that was played. Jon even choreographed dance routines for the newcomers before he was eight years old. Those were the days when visitors walked leisurely along the plank boardwalks and enjoyed the buildings that were furnished appropriately to the era. It was old-fashioned entertainment.

The day finally arrived for Dusty to play one of the leading roles in a gunfight. The last thing a group of young actors wants is for the audience to mistake them for amateurs. So to appease him, they promised that he could play the last act of the day, when the crowd would likely be smaller. What they hadn't counted on was that Dusty had slipped around and asked everyone to stay and watch his leading role as Grandpa. He played to a rip-roaring audience.

It was difficult to keep up with both Jon and Dusty. Despite their age difference, they were always pals. There were arm wrestles, war dances, riding the Honda 50 down Skaggs Creek, watering the horses, and battles on the river with toy boats and black gun powder. That last escapade sent Jon to the emergency room with weeks afterward of hand therapy. And once, from too much bleach applied by Betsy and from the swimming pool's chlorine, they both turned up at their sister Carcille's fashionable wedding with green-tinted hair.

One hot afternoon, little Betsy came bouncing through the front door of the store wearing one of her many self-assembled costumes— her brother's cowboy boots, too big and on the wrong feet, a long skirt dragging to her ankles and a fringed buckskin jacket zipped to her chin. Her hair was matted with Butch wax. We were accustomed to never knowing what to expect from this very happy child who sang songs, wandered around the doll table and finally approached the counter. For a wild moment I wanted to hide her. But Carlo whispered, "Don't even look at her. Maybe everyone will think she's a tourist."

Our river's landscape is still the same, just more lush and beautiful in its wild, undisturbed tranquility. Our view is glorious, green and forested with hemlock, poplar and sycamore trees. It's hard to describe the charm and magic of living on a river. It's been said that "forged with flooding waters, you will come back." I know now that real contentment comes from the ability to manifest your dreams. My days are now filled with satisfying work, greeting customers, loving friends and family members.

Every morning I open up the store, put things into their proper places, dust the displays and the countertops and check the phone messages. Then I go outside and water the plants. I see a hummingbird and several butterflies. A lizard darts back and forth on the steps. I watch the horses run and play. What, not another stray dog or cat!—but I feed them, and they become mine.

I look at the river to catch its color. I wave at passersby. The sun hits my favorite bench. I walk through the gardens, admiring the pretty flowers. My children call....

Acknowledgments

For the encouragement that has been given me from so many people to write this book ... I thank you.

It has been an incredible experience for me to relive the memory, to read to my friends, and to talk about a place that welcomes visitors who appreciate the natural beauty of the land. It's a work of art here – a reality, a way of life, and a dream that started over 50 years ago.

I want to make acknowledgments to certain individuals. Special thanks to Mary Jane French who typed and typed and typed. And to Laura Whitney Burchette who typed some more. I am grateful to Colleen Armstrong for her editing assistance, to Ann McCarthy for her early interest, Jean Baker Cobb for our family research, Jo Jo Rice and Jean Dewberry for listening to me read these stories over and over again. I am also grateful for excerpts from *The Ohio Long Rifle*, Chief R. Deerfoot's *Life of the Cherokee Indian Evangelist*, and Larue Paytiamo's *White Wife of a Red Man*; and for additional information from Tom B. Underwood's *The Story of the Cherokee People*. My thanks to Sharon Walker, Helen Norman, Carol Mills (*Sentinel Echo*) and Thomas Hart Shelby for providing photographs. Also, I want to thank the *Lexington Herald Leader* for the cover photo.

My greatest thanks, however, goes to each and every artisan who played a role on this stage that Carlo and I tried to create, and to the many, many visitors who have come into our store and traded over the years. Without them, there would be no story to tell.

To my parents, my grandmother Margaret B. Garrison, to Carlo and our children ... thank you for your love, and a beautiful journey.

INDEX